Collecting Stamps

COLLECTING STAMPS

Neil Grant and Peter Womersley

GRANADA
London Toronto Sydney New York

Granada Publishing Limited
Frogmore, St Albans, Herts AL2 2NF
and
3 Upper James Street, London W1R 4BP
866 United Nations Plaza, New York, NY 10017, USA
117 York Street, Sydney, NSW 2000, Australia
100 Skyway Avenue, Toronto, Ontario, Canada M9W 3A6
PO Box 84165, Greenside, 2034 Johannesburg, South Africa
61 Beach Road, Auckland, New Zealand

Published by Granada in 1980
Hardback ISBN 0 246 11327 8
Paperback ISBN 0 583 30387 0

Typeset by Georgia Origination, Liverpool

Printed and bound in Hong Kong by
Wing King Tong Co Ltd

Granada®
Granada Publishing®

Acknowledgements

The publishers are grateful to the following for supplying material for the illustrations in this book:

Peter Womersley; Stanley Gibbons International Ltd.; Harmers of London, Stamp Auctioneers; the Post Office, Publicity Department.

The Illustrations on p. 38 appear by courtesy of Bradbury, Wilkinson and Co. Ltd.; those on pp 12, 17, 18, 21, 24, 31, 33 by courtesy of the Post Office; on pp 15, 16, 20 and top 21, 28, 29 by courtesy of Harmers of London.

Stamp collecting equipment was kindly lent for photography by Stanley Gibbons International Ltd.

Contents

1
The Rise
of the
Post Office

Postage stamps as we know them today - little pieces of printed paper for sticking on letters - are a recent invention. They did not exist 150 years ago. The postal system itself is much older, but in the days before postage stamps it was a poor kind of system. Slow and unreliable, it was also very expensive. Most people then seldom wrote or received a letter. The easy communication by mail which we take for granted did not develop until after postage stamps were introduced.

Before that time, few people wanted to send letters. There were no birthday cards or Christmas cards, no seaside holidays for those wish-you-were-here cards. Most people lived in the same village or town all their lives. Their friends and relatives lived there too, and they had no need to correspond with another part of the country.

If they *could* correspond, that is. Most of them could neither read nor write. They were unable to send letters even if they wanted to.

All the same, from very early times some people did need to send messages a long distance. In the Bible, the Second Book of Chronicles tells of King Hezekiah, who 'sent word to all Israel and Judah, and also wrote letters to Ephraim and Manasseh, inviting them to come...to keep the Passover... Couriers went throughout all Israel and Judah with letters from the king and his officers...'

Kings and governors were the kind of people who needed to communicate quickly and at long distance. Naturally, they used their own servants as messengers. (And they still do: an ambassador going abroad carries letters from his or her government.)

Of course, sending out a group of messengers to deliver letters does not amount to a postal system. If King Hezekiah had wanted to send out new orders the following week, he would have had to start all over again. However, it was sometimes necessary to send many messages over the same route. A king at war in a foreign country might wish to communicate frequently and quickly with his capital. For that purpose, a relay system could be set up along the route, with each courier carrying the message one stage, then handing it on to the next.

During his invasion of Greece in the sixth century BC, the Persian king Xerxes (or Ahasuerus) kept in touch with Persia by an efficient courier system. 'There is nothing in the world which travels faster than these Persian couriers', wrote the Greek historian, Herodotus. 'The whole idea is a Persian invention and works like this: riders are stationed along the road, equal in number to the number of days the journey takes - a man and a horse for each day... The first, at the end of his stage, passes the dispatch to the second, the second to the third, and so on along the line...' Herodotus paid a famous tribute to the Persian couriers: 'Neither rain nor sun nor heat nor gloom of night stays these couriers from their appointed rounds.' These words now appear, carved in giant letters, on the General Post Office in New York City.

The Greeks themselves could send a message very quickly when necessary. The longest foot race in athletics today commemorates the feat of a runner who carried the news of the Greek victory at Marathon to Athens, a distance of nearly 23 miles (the modern marathon race is longer, 26 miles and 385 yards).

But for both kinds, 'footmen' and riders, it was a risky business. Apart from accidents, there was the danger of bandits or, in war time, enemy ambush. One Greek general used to write his messages on a kind of belt looped around a stick. When the stick was removed and the belt straightened out, the letters were jumbled up and the words could not be read by the enemy if the messenger were captured. But if the message were safely delivered, the belt was wrapped around another stick of the same size and the words then fell into place.

The first people in Europe to organize a genuine postal service were the Romans. As everyone knows, the Romans were great road-builders, and on some main roads in their empire they set up regular relays of horses and riders to carry the official dispatches of governors and generals in the provinces. They even had a service for parcels. Nothing like the Roman system existed again in Europe for over one thousand years after the Roman Empire had disappeared. In the Middle Ages, the Muslim world was more advanced in many ways than Christian Europe, and the Arabs ran a kind of postal service on certain well-travelled roads. They had an express service too. Ordinary letters - 'second-class mail' we might say - travelled at the plodding pace of the camel. 'First-class mail' was carried by the faster horse.

Although aeroplanes were not invented until the 20th century, airmail of a kind is almost as old as surface mail. Over two thousand years ago the Chinese used carrier pigeons to carry messages. The Romans too sometimes sent messages in little boxes tied to the legs of pigeons, and so did the Arabs. The Sultan of Baghdad established a pigeon post in 1150, and the rulers of Egypt in the 15th century had a pigeon relay which worked in the same way as the Roman relays of horses. They built pigeon lofts at intervals along the route.

It is strange how such ancient methods proved useful in much later times. Pigeons carried messages during the French revolution of 1848, and in the First World War they were used by secret agents behind the enemy lines. The United States army signal corps owned one long-winded pigeon which once carried a message 2,300 miles.

Pigeons were safe from attack by bandits. But unfortunately, they were not safe from hawks. Many a message in medieval Egypt was never delivered because the 'postman' had a fatal encounter with a peregrine falcon.

Nowadays, everyone has a simple address, usually the number of the house, the street, and the town. Those addresses make the postman's task easier, but until the nineteenth century no one had such a simple and clear address. If you wanted to say where you lived, you could name the town and possibly the street, but not the number of the house. Instead of saying, 'I live at No. 3, Hill Street', you might say, 'I live next to the grocer's shop' or 'near the sign of the clockmaker'. One letter in the fifteenth century was addressed 'To Thomas Greene, goodman of the George, by Powles Wharf, or to his wife, to send to Sir John Paston, wheresoever he be, at Calais, London, or other places'. Queen Elizabeth addressed a letter to the temporary sheriff of Kent like this: 'Our very loving friend the high sheriff for the time being of the County of Kent' (*Figure 1*). Addresses were long, but far from precise.

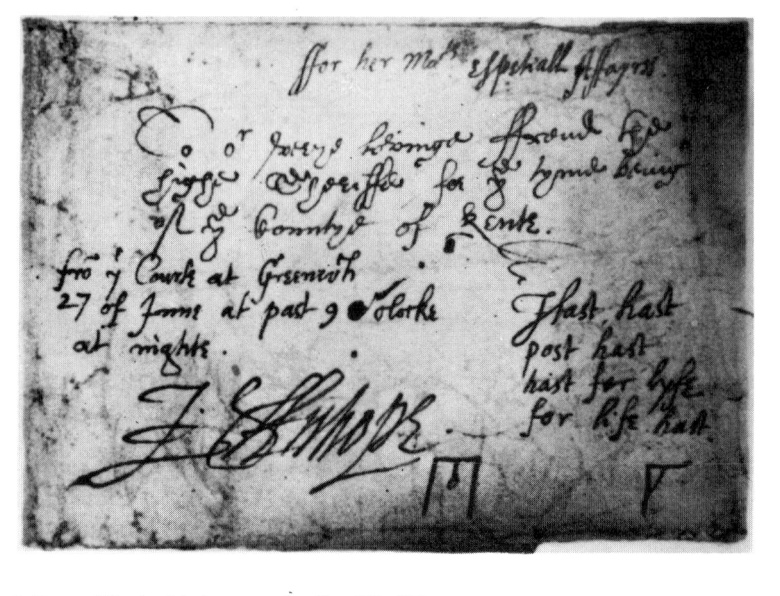

1 Queen Elizabeth's letter to the Sheriff of Kent

Greater accuracy was not really needed, because most letters went by special messenger, usually a servant of the sender, sometimes a passing traveller who agreed to deliver a letter for a fee.

The first country to establish a state post was probably France, in the fifteenth century. The English followed about half a century later when King Henry VIII appointed one of his officals 'master of the posts'. His job was to keep the King in contact with the capital at all times, and he set up a relay system on one or two main roads, with postmasters, in charge of forwarding the mail, along the route. The postmasters were usually inn-keepers, who could easily provide horses for royal couriers as they were already in business hiring horses to travellers. They also had to provide guides, for the roads were terrible and there were no signposts. Sometimes the mail packet was carried by postboys (not always boys despite their name), who were given a horse, a leather bag for the mail, and a horn to blow along the way to warn other travellers of their approach.

Besides the royal post, some private postal services existed, but we know very little about them. Merchants trading with foreign countries formed companies to conduct their business more easily, and some of these merchant companies ran a postal service for their members, with a weekly ship to the continent.

Governments never liked the idea of their subjects sending sealed letters to and fro. They suspected that plots were hatched and rebellions planned by such means. (Sometimes their suspicions were justified, although no doubt most letters were perfectly innocent.) Governments were therefore anxious to control all sending of messages, but that could only be done if governments themselves provided an efficient postal service. It was for this reason that the Post Office developed as a government department.

In 1660, the year when King Charles II was restored to the English throne after the upsets of the Civil War and the rule of Oliver Cromwell, an act of parliament established a national postal service. Unlike the earlier royal post, anyone could use it - for a fee. To send a letter of one sheet up to 80 miles cost two old pence (2d). More sheets or a greater distance and the price went up.

The official at the head of the Post Office was called the Postmaster General. He was not paid a salary, but himself paid the government an agreed sum in exchange for whatever profit he could make out of the posts. This way of conducting a government service, called 'farming', was quite common in the days when the civil service was very small. The Customs were also 'farmed' to a man who paid a lump sum to the government in return for pocketing customs duties. In the Holy Roman Empire, a very efficient postal system, with mounted postmen riding day and night, was farmed out to a well-known Austrian family for over 300 years.

The first Postmaster General after the act of 1660 was Colonel Bishop. He was the first in England to introduce a 'postmark'. It was made with a hand stamp, something like the rubber stamps in modern post offices, and stamped each letter with the 'Bishop mark' - a circle with a line dividing it. The upper half of the circle showed the month and the lower half the day of posting (*Figure 2*).

Although the act of 1660 said that all letters should be carried by the Post Office, private postal services still existed. London, in particular, had poor service. It was easier to send a letter from

London to Edinburgh than from one part of London to another. In 1680, therefore, a London merchant named William Dockwra introduced a local 'penny post' in the London area. He probably got the idea from the French, for the first local penny post was started in Paris in 1653.

Dockwra's penny post was highly efficient. He set up hundreds of places throughout the city where letters could be handed in, and guaranteed to deliver them within a few hours, or next day at the latest. Some receiving offices had twelve deliveries a day. Letters could also be delivered to the door, but that cost an extra penny. Like the Post Office, Dockwra used hand stamps to show where and when a letter was handed in, but his stamps showed the hour as well as the day (*Figures 3 & 4*).

After two years the Post Office took action to close down Dockwra's system. Soon afterwards, it paid him the compliment of setting up a similar local post for London, and put him in charge of it for a time.

One of the biggest drawbacks of the post at the end of the seventeenth century was that it was London-centred. Communication between London and any town on one of the five or six post roads which started there was good. They were not so good for a town not on a post road, and even worse between two provincial towns. Cross-country post routes were few. A letter from Stamford to Coventry (about 50 miles) had to travel via London (nearly 200 miles).

The man who put things right, one of the first great Post Office reformers, was Ralph Allen of Bath. He seems to have been an unusually nice man - kind, generous, honest and intelligent. Something of his character can be learned from *Tom Jones*, the novel by Allen's friend Henry Fielding, who put him into the book under the disguise of Squire Allworthy. As far as the history of the Post Office is concerned, however, Allen's most important quality was his skill at organization and administration. In 1720 he was put in charge of the by-posts or cross-posts, as they were called, the cross-country post roads. There were not many of them then, but by the time he died, over fifty years later, England was criss-crossed by a network of post roads joining all the major towns and cities. The income from the cross-posts in that time gives some idea of Allen's work. In 1727, when he had been in charge only seven

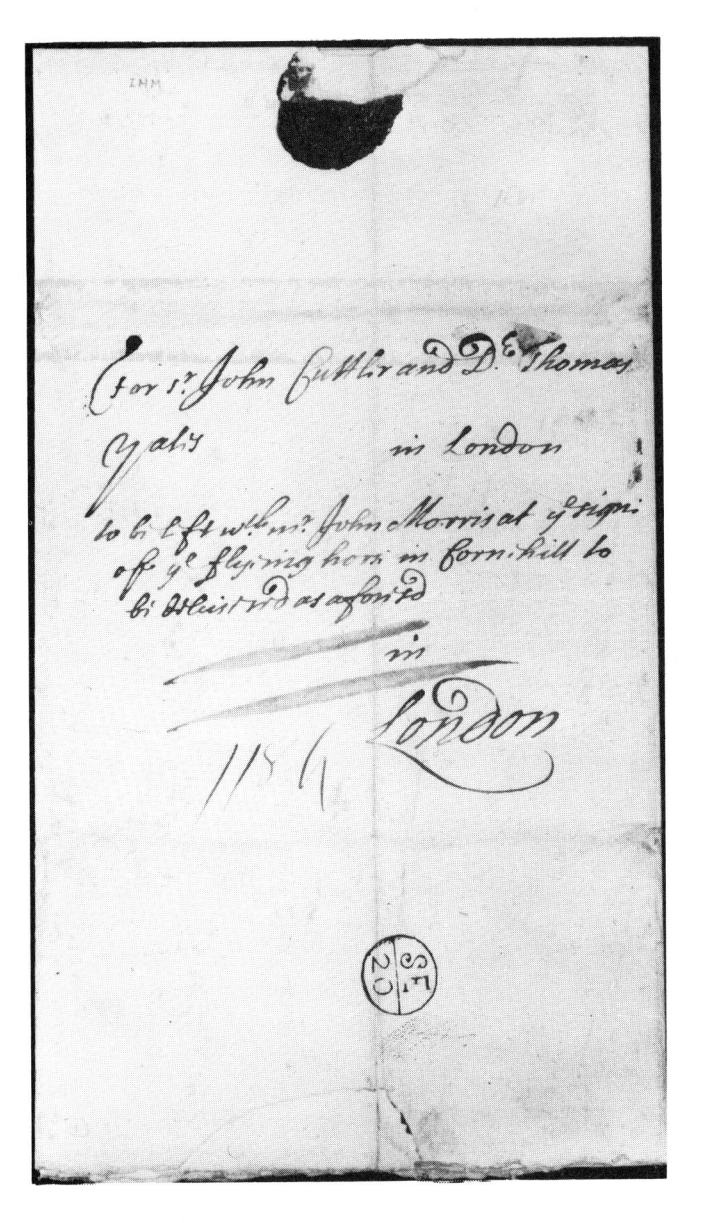

2 A letter with a Bishop postmark for 20 September

3 Two Dockwra postmarks showing the time posted; below the London mark

years, the cross-posts earned just over £2,000. By 1760, they were earning over £32,000. Allen also increased the number of posts. In 1720 many places had only one delivery a week. By 1760 daily deliveries were common.

The postboys who carried the mailbags were slow and unreliable. They were easily robbed, and some of them were in league with the robbers. The Post Office advised customers sending bank notes or cash drafts by post to cut the notes in half and send one half only. When they heard that the packet had arrived safely, they could send the other half.

In the late eighteenth century, travel by road was getting easier. Improvements in the roads themselves and the rise of the four-horse stage-coach made journeys swifter and safer. On the main

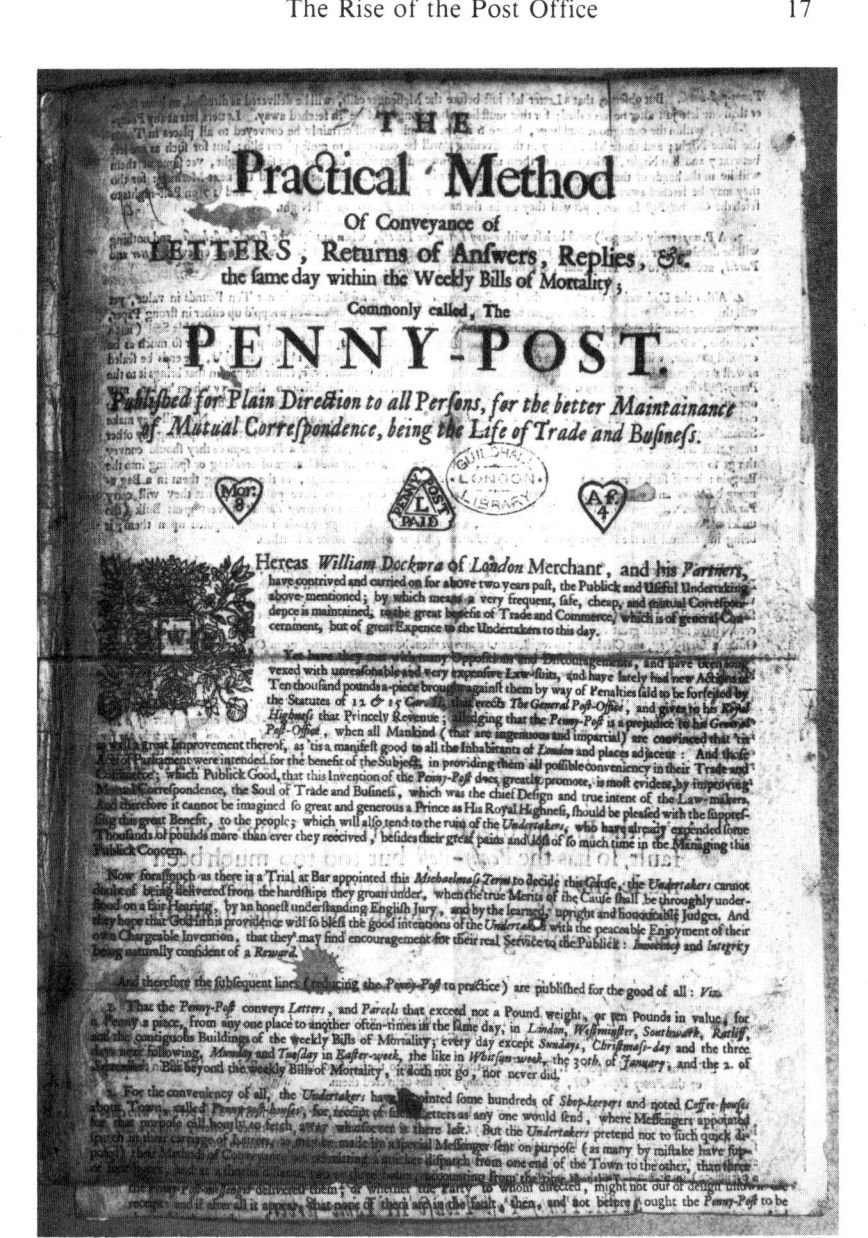

4 Advertisement for Dockwra's London penny post, about 1681

5 The Dover mail, about 1837. The mail bags were exchanged without stopping the horses

roads, stage-coaches travelled more than twice as fast as postboys, and many people were tempted to send their letters by the stage-coach, although it was more expensive as well as illegal.

To John Palmer, a businessman who, like Ralph Allen, came from Bath, this was an absurd situation. He suggested a new plan for carrying the mail by special mail-coaches, which would go as fast, or faster, than the privately owned stage-coaches.

Like other postal reformers, Palmer ran into powerful opposition, and the fiercest critics of his plan were the Post Office officials themselves. They raised all kinds of objections, but probably the real reason for their opposition was the ordinary, human dislike of changes. They had been running things in the old way for many years, and they resented someone like Palmer, who had no connection with the Post Office, jumping up and saying it should all be done differently. However, Palmer persuaded the prime minister, William Pitt, that his scheme would work, and in 1784 the first mail-coach ran from Bristol to London. Not only was it far faster than the postboys, it knocked an hour or so off the time taken by the stage-coach.

Within a few years mail-coaches, built to a special design approved by Palmer, were running on all the main roads from London to the provinces and between some other cities as well. Palmer's system brought an enormous improvement. Someone in Bristol or Norwich writing a letter to London in 1784 was lucky to receive a reply within a week. After the mail-coach began running, a letter sent on Monday would be answered by Wednesday (*Figure 5*).

Some other improvements were made in the Post Office during the Palmer era, but one thing that Palmer's methods did not do was to bring down the cost of postage. In fact postage became more expensive. To send a letter of a single sheet from London to Edinburgh cost over a shilling (5p), equivalent to several pounds today.

The Post Office was not making as much money as it ought. One reason was various forms of cheating, such as sending letters by illegal carriers. Though the population was increasing fast and more letters were being written in the early years of the 19th century, the number of letters handled by the Post Office actually decreased.

Parliament ordered several investigations of the Post Office, and a number of reforms were suggested. One way in which money could be saved was by reducing the salaries of the top officials. The Postmaster General, for example, was usually some idle peer who sat in the House of Lords, drew a large salary, and left all the work to others.

Newspapers were also costing the Post Office a fortune because they travelled free. They did have to pay a tax, but the tax did not go to the Post Office. When the tax was reduced from 4d to 1d in 1836, a great many more newspapers were published - and posted free.

Worst of all was the scandal of the 'free frank'. All members of parliament, and some other fortunate individuals, had the right of free postage. They had only to put their signature, or 'frank', on the front of the letter and no charge was made (*Figure 6*). If MPs had used their privilege for their own letters only, it would not have made much difference to Post Office revenue. But on the contrary, they willingly franked the letters of anyone else, usually accepting a fee for doing so. One MP was paid £300 a year by a single business company for franking their letters. In 1784 the Post Office

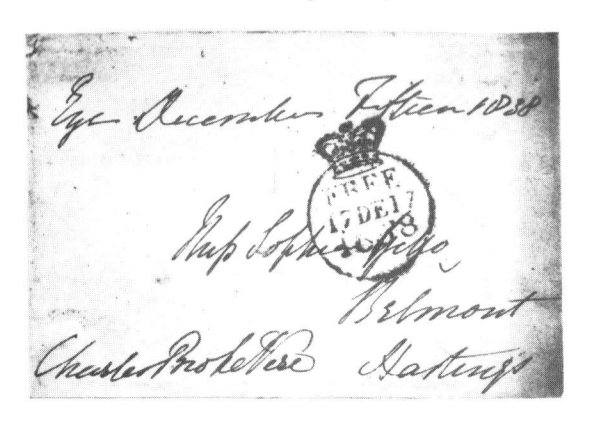

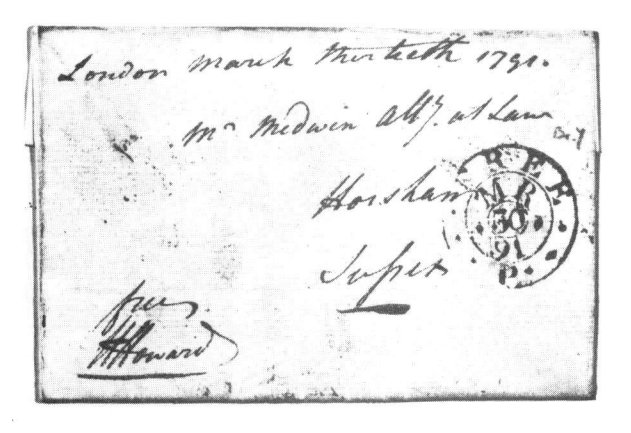

6 Letters mailed under a free frank in the early 19th century

7 A postman taking payment for delivering a letter

estimated that the amount of money it lost through the free frank was almost equal to the total revenue from inland mail.

The methods of the Post Office itself were very inefficient, and therefore expensive. Postage on letters did not have to be paid at the time of posting, and by far the greatest number were paid for on delivery, by the person receiving the letter rather than the person writing it. This wasted a great deal of time, as the postman had to wait to be paid for every letter he delivered. Some people, moreover, were unwilling to pay. A working man had to think hard before he paid out 8d or 1 shilling for a letter. That was almost as much as he earned for a day's work (*Figure 7*).

Many people invented clever ways of avoiding postage charges. A person going abroad would arrange a code with his family. On his letters he would write the address in a certain way - perhaps altering the spelling slightly - according to the message he wanted to send. Each variation would mean something different in the pre-arranged code. When the letter arrived and the postman asked for payment, the family would ask to see the letter, examine the address, then hand it back saying they were unable to pay for it. They had of course already learned that their relative was in London and in good health,. or in Paris and in need of money or whatever message was concealed in the way the address was written.

2
The
Penny Post

By the early nineteenth century the Post Office needed thorough reform. A few people stood up and said so, and the general public responded with enthusiasm. Post Office reform, or 'cheap postage', became a popular cause.

Popular with the public, it was not so popular with MPs and government officials who feared the loss of the free frank. If it had been left to government alone - MPs and civil servants - the Penny Post would certainly have been delayed. But public opinion was behind the reformers, and by the 1830s public opinion was not so easily ignored by the government as it was a generation earlier. Not every member of the ruling class, of course, was against cheap postage. Queen Victoria, whose opinions on many subjects were more liberal than those of her ministers, was in favour of it. In the reformed parliament elected after the act of 1832, several MPs supported Post Office reform, especially Robert Wallace, the member for Greenock. His first speech in the House of Commons was a terrific attack on the administration of the Post Office.

The man who took the lead in the fight for Post Office reform was neither an M.P. nor a Post Office official. He was a civil servant with a gift for figures and a powerful ambition to get ahead in the world. Rowland Hill saw the need for Post Office reform and made that his life's work. In later years he could hardly talk about any other subject. As his son once told him, when he reached the gates of Heaven he would undoubtedly ask St Peter about postal arrangements up there (*Figure 8*).

The Post Office kept Mr. Hill at arm's length, refusing to allow him inside the doors to do his research. However, he was able to get all the information he needed from government publications, which were sent to him by his ally in parliament, Robert Wallace. So bulky were these documents that they had to be delivered to

8 Rowland Hill in 1890

Hill's house in a horse-drawn cab. They were delivered free by the Post Office, because Wallace, as an M.P., had a free frank.

With Wallace's help, Hill wrote his pamphlet on *Post Office Reform* (1837), the 'bible' of the cheap-postage movement. It analysed the Post Office in careful detail and provided evidence in support of two basic reforms: first, that postage should be paid in advance; second, that there should be a low, standard rate of postage, with no extra charge for distance.

Hill showed that the system of payment on delivery was an enormous waste of time. If postage were already paid, the postman could simply deliver the letters at each house, completing his round in a fraction of the time. Hill suggested that householders should make slits in their doors so the postman would not have to knock and wait for an answer (there were no letterboxes then).

Secondly, Hill argued that huge savings in time and money could be made by a low, standard rate of postage. Under the system as it was then, the clerk in the receiving office had to examine each letter carefully. First he looked at the address to see how far it had to go, then calculated the postage payable for that distance. Then he had to examine it to see how many sheets it contained, perhaps going over to the window to hold it up to the light. Finally, having calculated the distance and the number of sheets, he wrote or stamped on the letter the postage that had to be paid when it was delivered.

Some of Hill's supporters showed how absurd this method was by posting two letters with the same address. The first was an extremely bulky packet made up of a single enormous sheet of paper. The second was tiny, but contained two small, thin sheets. The postage for the second was twice as much as the postage for the large packet, because it contained two sheets.

Instead of charging for the number of sheets, it was obviously more sensible, as Hill said, to charge according to the weight of the letter. This system was already in use in France and some other countries.

Hill made some skilful calculations by which he was able to demonstrate that the distance a letter travelled made very little difference to the cost. The cost to the Post Office of sending a letter from London to Edinburgh according to Hill's calculations, was just $1/36$ of one penny, and of course most letters travelled at much shorter distance. Far the largest proportion of the cost was in handling the letter at either end, and that was the same whether the letter was going four miles or four hundred.

Hill's main opponents, as John Palmer might have warned him, were the officials of the Post Office. The Postmaster General had this to say of *Post Office Reform*: 'Of all the wild and visionary schemes I have ever heard or read of, it is the most extravagant'.

But popular support for his idea was enormous. The pressure of public opinion was so great that in 1839 parliament passed an act to put into effect all the changes that Hill and the reformers demanded.

Postage charges were to be lowered and based on the weight of the letter only. The act did not actually say that the charge would be one penny, as Hill suggested in his pamphlet, but after all the publicity for a Penny Post it would have been difficult to get any higher charge. The free frank nonsense was swept away; even Queen Victoria gave up the sovereign's right to free postage (though Edward VII was to get it back). Finally, the act said that some form of stamped paper should be provided for the pre-payment of postage. The act went into effect in January 1840, when a letter weighing up to ½ ounce could be posted anywhere in Britain for one penny.

The splendid new G.P.O. building in St Martin's-le-Grand in London (since pulled down) was crowded with people in January 1840. Some came just to look, but many came to take advantage of the new, cheap postage. Normally, there was one clerk at one window to receive letters for posting. But, expecting a rush, the Post Office had opened six windows, with two clerks at each one. As closing time approached, yet another window had to be opened, and at last, to make sure that no one should be turned away, the postmaster opened an eighth window. As all the clerks were busy, he manned it himself. When the office closed, the crowd gave two cheers, one for the Post Office and one for Rowland Hill.

At this time, the price of postage was still stamped or written on the letter in the old way. The act of parliament had confirmed that postage should be prepaid (it was still possible to pay on delivery but the cost was twice as much), but when the Penny Post began, a method for pre-payment of postage had not yet been settled. There was still no such thing as an adhesive postage stamp. One suggestion was for a kind of printed envelope, which could be bought in advance from the Post Office. This system already existed in parts of Italy. Another possibility was suggested by Hill: 'A piece of paper just large enough to bear the stamp (i.e. postmark) and covered at the back with a glutinous wash, which the bringer might, by applying a little moisture, attach to the ... letter'. Without knowing it, Hill had described the modern, adhesive postage stamp. In later years he always claimed that stamps were his idea, but in fact so many ideas were floating about at the time that we cannot be certain that Hill was the true inventor of the stamp. James Chalmers, a newspaper publisher in Dundee, seems to have had the idea as early as 1834.

Neither Hill nor anyone else realized that the postage stamp would prove to be the best answer to the problem of prepaid postage. He thought the printed cover would probably be more effective, but the public preferred the sticky stamp.

Like all prophets of change, Hill made some mistakes. Underestimating the postage stamp was one of them. Another was his calculation of the Post Office's profits. The average price for posting a letter in 1839 was 8d, so the introduction of the Penny Post meant in effect that the cost of postage was reduced by 800 per cent. Hill said that the increase in the number of letters, together with the easier methods of posting, would make up for that enormous reduction; Post Office revenue, he believed, would not suffer. In fact, it fell by two-thirds. Not for many years did the net income of the Post Office under the Penny Post system equal its income before 1840. The one-penny rate was really too low at that time. It would probably have been wiser to fix it at 2d, but people had got used to the idea of a Penny Post. Not only was it the battle cry of the reformers, it already existed in many towns for local letters only.

The first postage stamp was the famous Penny Black (*Figure 9*). Among the hundreds of thousands of stamps issued throughout the world since 1840, few if any have been coloured black. The reason

9 A Penny Black (*enlarged*)

10 A Maltese Cross postmark on British 2d blue stamps

is obvious: the cancellation stamp, or postmark, would not show up on a black postage stamp. However, in 1840 the Post Office cancelled the stamps in red ink. Experience showed that the red ink could be removed rather easily, allowing dishonest people to use the stamp again. Black ink proved harder to erase, but it did not show up on a black postage stamp. The answer was to change the colour of the stamp, and the Penny Black was replaced by a brownish red.

The stamps were originally cancelled with a mark like a Maltese Cross (*Figure 10*). But that did not show the time and place of posting, and it was soon replaced by a number. Each postal town was given its own identity number, and this figure stamped on a letter showed where it had been posted. Soon, most towns adopted a circular postmark, like those still used today, which gave the place, date and time of posting (*Figure 11*).

Naturally, the Penny Post resulted in a lot more letters being posted. In 1839, the last year of the old system, the Post Office delivered about 75 million letters. In 1840, the first year of the Penny Post, the total was more than doubled, and by 1870 it had risen to 880 million.

The introduction of the Penny Post in Britain established the basic service for letters that we have today. Other countries were quick to follow Britain's example. Brazil and the Swiss canton (province) of Zurich were among the first, introducing cheap standard rates in 1843. But, like other countries, they profited from the mistakes as well as the improvements made in Britain. Switzerland, for example, had two rates of postage within each canton, one for short and one for long-distance deliveries, while Brazil fixed its standard rate at more than twice the British penny.

11 A letter bearing a Penny Black stamp posted in 1841

The United States was particularly interested in the movement for postal reform in Britain in the late 1830s and sent a special observer to keep an eye on developments there. When he returned, he recommended two rates for postage in the United States: 5 cents for the first 500 miles and 10 cents for a longer distance (a U.S. cent was then equal to a halfpenny). But when cheap postage went into effect in the United States in 1845, the 5-cent post was limited to 300 miles. In 1863 a single rate came into effect for the whole country, but not until twenty years later was it reduced to a penny - actually 2 cents. The first official U.S. postage stamps were issued in 1847.

Besides Britain, the European country with the most advanced postal arrangements was France. The French were quick to introduce a standard rate of postage which, with their eyes on the diminished revenue of the British Post Office, they set at the equivalent of 2d, and pre-payment was made compulsory in France earlier than Britain. The first French postage stamps, however, were not issued until 1849.

The French also invented the pillar box. In Britain letters had to be taken to the post office or given to one of the 'bellmen', who walked the streets ringing a bell and carrying a large bag with a slit in the top for letters (*Figure 12*). The first pillar box in Britain was erected in the Channel Islands at the suggestion of Anthony Trollope, a Post Office official for most of his life though better known as a novelist. Rowland Hill used to insist that the pillar box was his idea, but in his later years Hill was inclined to believe that any useful idea connected with the post had originally been his.

Pillar boxes, first seen in London in 1855, were a novelty that some people did not like (*Figure 13*). Trollope wrote about one old lady who said that she would not trust the things with her letters and always took them to the post office. Probably there were many like her. The owner of a business company in the 1850s complained to the Post Office that none of his firms's letters ever reached their destination. The clerks scratched their heads and puzzled over the disappearing mail for weeks. It turned out that the company's office boy, a simple-minded youth, had been 'posting' all the letters in a disused water pump which he thought was one of the new pillar boxes.

Not all the good ideas came from Britain or France. The postcard, for example, seems to have been invented in Austria, another country with a distinguished postal tradition. What made the postcard really popular was the development of photography and hence the picture postcard. Some old Victorian postcards are very interesting, or at least quaint, and today many people collect old

12 A 'bellman'. Letters could be posted in his bag in the days before pillar boxes

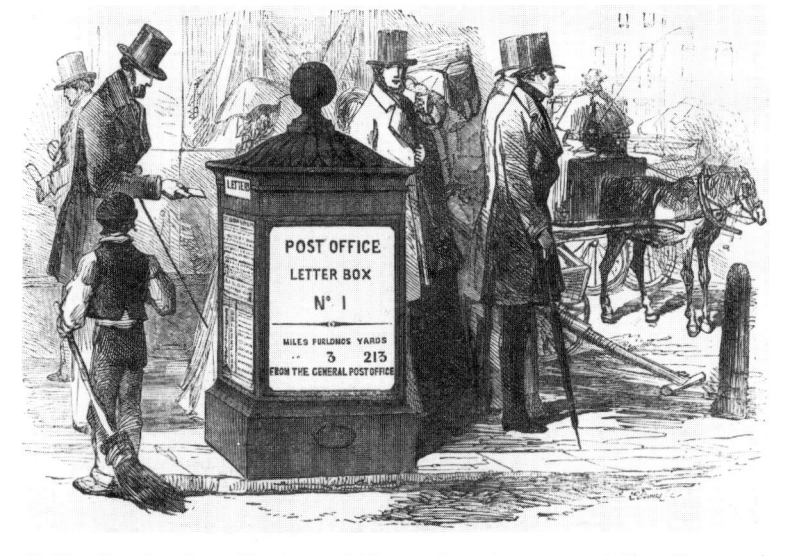

13 The first London pillar box, which stood on the corner of Fleet Street and Farringdon Street

postcards just as others collect stamps.

By the time the Penny Post began, the dashing red-and-black mail coaches had virtually all disappeared from the main roads. A few survived on minor routes; in parts of Scotland the mail was still carried by coach in the early twentieth century. But in general the mail went by train. On long routes it was actually sorted in a travelling post office in one of the carriages. The railway was of course faster, though not necessarily cheaper. The Post Office had many a battle with the railway companies over their charges, and this was the main reason why a parcel service did not begin in Britain until 1883. Many other countries had a parcel post earlier than that, although in the United States, where private carriers fought a long battle against the Post Office, parcel post did not begin until 1912.

The steam engine also helped to improve foreign mails, as steamboats crossed the oceans faster and more reliably than sailing ships. Many countries made arrangements to handle each other's mail, and in 1875 a general, international agreement was reached with the foundation of the Universal Postal Union, to which nearly all countries belong nowadays. The man who, more than anyone else, was responsible for the creation of the UPU was the German postal reformer, Heinrich von Stephan, Germany's Rowland Hill, as he is sometimes called. Basically, the members of the UPU agreed to handle each other's mail when it entered their territory exactly as if it was their own. The UPU also made international postage simpler by issuing rules governing rates and such matters as the colour of the most common stamps.

Since the middle of the nineteenth century, the work of the Post Office has been greatly enlarged and improved. Registered mail began under Rowland Hill, though an unofficial system of registered mail, run by the post office clerks, already existed. An express or 'special delivery' service was started in Britain in 1891.

In the last twenty or thirty years, the main changes in the Post Office, as in many other institutions, have been in mechanization - getting machines to do the work previously done by hand (*Figure 14*). Many countries have introduced postal codes, a number added to the address on a letter, which makes it possible for one man - and a machine - to do the work which previously kept a dozen people

14 An automatic letter-sorting machine, which can sort 9,000 letters an hour

occupied. The Post Office has always been what is called a 'labour-intensive' industry; in other words, it depends very largely on human labour. In these days of rising wages it has become necessary to reduce labour costs as far as possible, and mechanization is therefore inevitable (though no one has invented a machine to replace the postman who delivers the letters to the door). In some ways it has brought greater efficiency. On the whole, it has helped to keep postal rates down, for the rising cost of postage, which has left the Penny Post far behind, is due more to general inflation than the Post Office raising prices. But modern advantages have not really improved postal deliveries. Someone observed that in 1979, despite airmail and mechanization, it took longer for a letter from Britain to reach certain countries abroad than it did in the 18th century. The deteriorating service, which was partly the result of temporary difficulties such as a shortage of staff, was beginning to worry many people. For it is hard to over-estimate our dependence today on the remarkable services which the Post Office provides.

3
How Stamps
are Made

The reason why most people start collecting postage stamps in the first place is that they are attracted by their appearance - their small size, bright colours, varied designs and so on. The attractive appearance of stamps may be enough to satisfy some people, but most collectors sooner or later become interested in the methods by which stamps are produced. Just as someone who is interested in cars wants to know how the engine works, most stamp collectors like to know something about the design and printing of stamps. Some experts and specialists study this part of the subject very closely, but for the average collector a little background knowledge is enough.

Stamp collectors often first become interested in the production process when they come across an error in a stamp, or a small difference between two stamps which are otherwise alike. Errors can occur at any stage - perhaps when the stamps are being designed, perhaps when they are being printed - and small changes may be made deliberately for a new printing of an old issue. The collector will want to know how and why these errors or changes happened.

Once it has been decided to issue a new stamp or set of stamps, the Post Office authorities commission an artist to make a preliminary design. Often they will ask several artists to submit designs and choose the one they like best. The artist is told what must appear on the stamp - the name of the country, the denomination or value, and probably what the picture should show. For example, if the stamp is to commemorate a certain famous person or a particular event, the artist will be told to draw a picture of that person or event. He or she may also be told what printing method will be used, as this may influence the type of design, and possibly the colours of the stamps (*Figure 15*).

15 Philip Sharland working on the design for a British stamp commemorating the 200th anniversary of the United States Declaration of Independence

When these instructions have been received, the artist can begin. His first job is research - to ensure that any technical or historical details in the design are correct. Mistakes can easily happen here. The design of the St Kitts-Nevis and Anguilla stamp, based on the islands' coat of arms, showed Christopher Columbus looking through a telescope a hundred years before telescopes were invented (*Figure 36d*). There have been many mistakes of this kind: the flag of the United States with the wrong number of stars, or the Nicaraguan stamp which showed the president of Nicaragua making a speech to the U.S. Congress in the House of Representatives instead of the Senate. In this case, the designer had based the scene on a photograph, but had been given a photograph of the wrong chamber.

When he knows exactly what will appear in it, the artist begins his drawing. He does not make his design the same size as the final postage stamp but three or four times larger. He may make several alternative designs, which are printed, usually in one colour only, and submitted to the postal authorities. These trial designs are called 'essays'. The design chosen is next photographed and reproduced in the correct, postage-stamp size, to make sure the words and figures are readable and the details clear. The artist may be asked to make some small changes in the design at this stage.

All this may take months, but at last the final design is ready. The next step is to transfer it on to some kind of surface, usually metal, for printing.

The earliest stamps were produced by *line engraving* or *recess printing*, still a very good method. The design is first engraved, in reverse, on a small metal block called a die. The parts of the design which are to be printed are cut away and the non-printing parts left at the original level, so that the pattern is sunk or 'recessed'. The master die is then duplicated fifty or a hundred times on a metal plate. When the actual printing takes place, the ink is forced into the cut-away portions by rollers and wiped off the raised surfaces. The plate and paper are pressed together, and the recessed parts containing ink are reproduced on the paper.

The chief difference between this method and *surface printing* or *typographic printing* is that in surface printing the non-printing parts of the die (and therefore of the printing plate in turn) are cut away, leaving the printing parts raised. When the rollers apply the ink, it is left on the raised parts only. The process works in exactly the same way as an office rubber stamp, which is pressed into an ink pad and then stamped on the paper.

In *lithography* or *offset printing*, the printing surface is entirely flat. The design is transferred to the printing surface (originally stone but more often specially treated metal) in some kind of greasy medium. The plate is then moistened and, as grease repels water, only the non-printing areas become wet. Rollers carrying the ink or pigment are rotated over the plate and, as this ink or pigment is also greasy, it does not stick to the wet parts of the plate. When the plate is brought into contact with the paper, only the inked parts make an impression.

Printing is a complicated craft which requires a long apprenticeship to learn, and there are many variations of these three basic methods. Modern forms of printing often make use of photography in some way, and probably the most common method of printing stamps today is by *photogravure*.

Photogravure is really a form of recess printing. Basically, a photograph of the design is transferred to a copper cylinder, and the printing parts are etched ('bitten out') in the copper by acid. The darker areas of the design are etched more deeply than the lighter parts; therefore, they collect more ink and come out darker on the printed paper when the cylinder is rolled over it. In reality, the whole process is much more complicated and includes many more stages than this short description.

Some early stamps were *embossed*, which means the pattern of the stamp is made in dents and ridges - you can feel them by running your finger over the surface. This is done by using two dies, one of them with the design engraved in recess and the other with the design raised. Thus they fit into each other, and when the paper is pressed between them the slight three-dimensional effect is created.

Most printing today is done on rotary presses, with a printing plate curved around a cylinder instead of being flat. A different cylinder is used for each colour of the stamp. Printers have to be especially careful when mixing the coloured inks to make sure they have the correct colour, shade and consistency. The temperature and the humidity must also be watched, as very warm or cold conditions may affect the result. It is important, too, that the sheets are placed in exactly the right position when several colours are being printed, otherwise the colours will overlap the edges of the areas where they should appear (*Figure 16*).

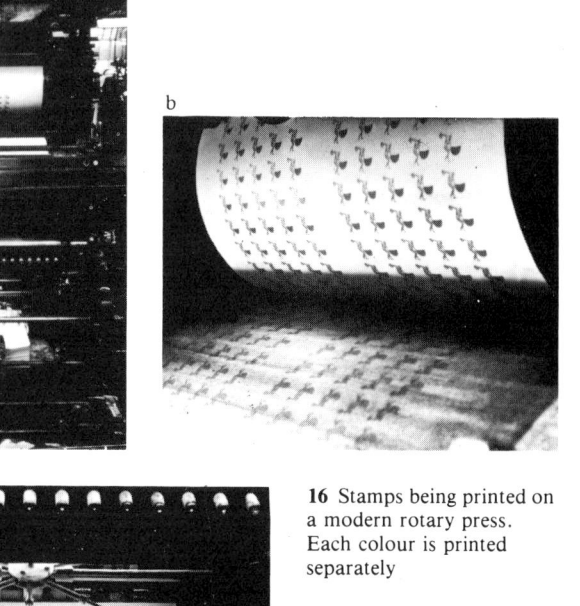

16 Stamps being printed on a modern rotary press. Each colour is printed separately

When the sheets have been printed, dried and checked, the lines of perforation are made between the individual stamps. Finally, the adhesive gum is applied to the back of the sheets. This used to be done by a man with a paste pot, and a large brush, but nowadays, of course, it is done mechanically.

Most stamps were, and are, produced by one of the methods described above. However, sometimes very unusual methods have been adopted, often because a national emergency made normal printing impossible. During the seven-month siege of Mafeking (1899-1900) during the South African War, stamps were produced by simple photography. More recently, some stamps in Tonga were made by stamping a pattern in metal foil. In Uganda in 1895, when there were no stamps or printing presses, a missionary named Millar made some stamps on his own typewriter: it took only an hour or so to produce enough stamps for local needs, and today these typewritten stamps of Uganda are very rare. There are other examples of 'home-made' stamps, like those of New Caledonia in 1860. The commanding officer of that remote French colony in the Pacific thought that the island should have its own stamps for local postage and asked one of his sergeants to make some. Sergeant Triquérat of the French Marines had no equipment at all, but he was an enterprising man. He sharpened the point of a nail, dipped it in greasy ink and on a flat stone he drew five rows of ten stamps each. He copied his design roughly from the stamps on the mail from France, which bore the head of the Emperor Napoleon III. These primitive lithographed stamps of New Caledonia were soon fetching high prices among collectors who would not have paid a fraction of the price for many more beautifully printed stamps.

4
The Growth
of a
Hobby

Nearly a century and a half have passed since the first postage stamp, the famous Penny Black of Great Britain, was issued. Since then, thousands of different postage stamps have been issued by countries all over the world. Today, postage stamps are among the commonest of everyday objects.

Since that day in May 1840, millions of people of all ages and nationalities have collected postage stamps àt some time in their lives. How did it all begin? Obviously, in 1840 or 1841 no one thought of collecting stamps, as there were hardly any to collect. However, stamp collecting began very soon. As early as 1845, a magazine in Germany reported:

In England, which has a very insignificant yet regular postal service, the Post Office sells small square pieces of paper bearing the head of the Queen, and these are stuck on the letter to be franked. In this simple manner the postage due is paid... The Queen's head looks very pretty and the English reveal their strange character by collecting these stamps.

So, by 1845 at least, the English were collecting stamps, and thus helping to convince other nations of what they had always suspected, that the English were crazy.

Two or three years earlier, several advertisements had been placed in *The Times* by ladies asking for old postage stamps. One lady was trying to paper her room with Penny Blacks. Another said she had been promised £3,000 if she succeeded in collecting 720,000 stamps. But the first people who began collecting as a hobby were probably young children, who were fascinated by the little printed labels on the letters brought by the postman. That, no doubt, explains why stamp collecting in the early days was not generally taken very seriously.

Within about twenty years, that attitude had changed. A French magazine published an article about stamps in 1862, which said that many old stamps could then only be bought for about 100 times their original value. Obviously, children could not afford such prices. Stamp collecting had been taken up seriously.

The original Penny Blacks and Twopence Blues of Britain had been printed with different letters in the bottom corners of each stamp, so that every stamp on a sheet of 240 was different. Some people tried to collect a complete sheet, first, perhaps, of Penny Blacks, then of Twopence Blues. Then, having caught the 'collector's disease', they started to collect stamps from other countries. Soon, stamp collecting became not just a children's amusement, but the serious hobby of wealthy men. For some reason, it became especially popular with royalty, perhaps because kings and queens have more spare time than most people, perhaps because a stamp collection is a valuable and easily transportable investment. A king who was overthrown by a revolution could easily pack his stamp collection to take with him on his flight into exile. It was not such an easy matter to take the furniture or the Crown Jewels. George V of England was one famous stamp collector. Of course, he never had to flee the throne, and his collection is still owned by the present Queen. King Farouk of Egypt was another collector, but when he was driven out of his country in an army revolt led by Colonel Nasser, he left his stamp collection behind.

Kings and millionaires have formed some of the most valuable collections. When Alfred H. Caspary of New York died in 1955, his collection was sold. It took sixteen separate auctions to sell it all, and the total amount paid was nearly $3 million. Another famous collection was sold by the New York banker, Marc Haas, to Stanley Gibbons, the British stamp dealers, in 1979. Although it was not a particularly large collection, it contained many very rare items and Stanley Gibbons paid $10 million for it.

These are very unusual examples, which have little to do with the ambitions of the average stamp collector. To make a collection today like the Caspary or Haas collection would be all but impossible, and would certainly require great knowledge, much time, some luck, and a vast amount of cash.

One sign of the respectability of stamp collecting as a serious occupation was the invention of a scientific name for it, *philately*.

It was formed from two Greek words, *philos*, meaning loving, and *ateleia*, meaning free from tax. Letters with postage prepaid by a stamp were 'free from tax', so a philatelist is someone who loves the things which signify freedom from tax. It is easy to understand how serious collectors who studied stamps in a scientific way wanted a word to describe this interest which was different from the name commonly given to a child's hobby. All the same, they might have thought of something less clumsy and less obscure. The man who is said to have invented the word in 1865, George Herpin, was a Frenchman, but the French also have another and better word, *timbrologie*, meaning 'the study of stamps'.

No one has ever given a satisfactory answer to the question, 'Why do people collect stamps?' The collecting urge, whether it is stamps, coins, pictures or anything else, seems to exist in most people, and stamps have many advantages as collectable objects. They are fairly easy to obtain, they do not take up much room and they do not require much expensive equipment. They are also colourful and exotic, sometimes bearing the names of countries you have heard of but are never likely to visit, and displaying an endless variety of little pictures. They provide easy, introductory lessons in world geography or history. They may well prove a good investment, since the value of some (by no means all) stamps goes up faster than the rate of inflation. But few people take up this hobby because they want to make a profit out of it, and it would be unwise to collect stamps for that reason alone. There are many more reliable ways of making money.

The truth is that there is no single reason for collecting stamps. If you asked a hundred stamp collectors why they collect, you would probably get a hundred different answers. Each person has his own preferences and his own interests. He or she decides what he wants to collect and in what way. There are few set rules that have to be followed in stamp collecting, and that is one reason why it appeals to so many people. There is almost nothing that you *must* do when you collect stamps, although there are a number of things you must *not* do if you are to get the most satisfaction from your hobby and if you wish to spend your money in the wisest way. This book is intended to provide, for new collectors as well as for someone who has been collecting for some time, useful information on how best to develop and look after a collection.

5
Starting a
Stamp
Collection

Many young people are attracted to the stamps they see on letters coming into their homes and decide to start saving the different ones that come their way. A collection of the current stamps of the country can be built up quite quickly, and friends and relatives can be asked to save the stamps on any letters or postcards they receive from abroad. It sometimes happens that an older member of the family has an old stamp collection which he or she is willing to give away. In that case the new collector is off to a flying start. But most people have to begin by picking up the odd stamp here and there. In that way a small but interesting collection can be gradually formed.

As time goes on it will become increasingly difficult to add new specimens to this kind of collection. The collector will want to expand, and it becomes necessary to spend some money.

A good way to start is by buying a stamp collector's outfit. These outfits usually contain a stamp album to contain the stamps, hinges for mounting them in the album, tweezers for handling them, and a large packet of different stamps from a variety of countries. These stamps must be sorted into countries and then into sets (groups of stamps belonging to the same issue) or part sets. The collection is now taking serious shape. The collector has learned to identify the stamps of many countries and knows something already about the different denominations or values. He or she is on the way to becoming a *philatelist*.

The next step is to buy a larger packet of mixed stamps to add to those already in the collection. Some stationery and book shops as well as stamp dealers sell packets of 'all different' stamps of the world. Some of the stamps will probably be the same as those already in the album. They can be put to one side; they may be useful later in exchanging with other collectors.

By this time the collection probably contains several hundred stamps from around the world. Some countries will be better represented than others, and it is time now to become more selective before buying. Perhaps there are no stamps on the page headed 'Canada', for example, or perhaps the collector already feels a special interest in Canadian stamps. In either case, a good way to increase the collection of a particular country is to visit the same stamp shop as before and this time buy a packet of stamps of that country only. The stamp dealer will be able to offer packets of 10, 20, or 50 Canada, or most other large countries. These packets are not expensive.

A general collection of all the countries in the world has a lot to recommend it. The main drawback is that, with hundreds of countries issuing new stamps every few months, only someone with millions to spend could attempt to keep up with all the current issues, never mind the older and rarer stamps. The serious collector usually finds sooner or later that a general collection is simply too large. He decides to specialize, perhaps by concentrating on the stamps of one country or, perhaps by collecting certain kinds of' stamp only.

Specialization can take many forms. Many stamp collectors call themselves 'specialists when they decide to give up their general collection and concentrate only on, for example, the stamps of the United States or the British Empire. Later on, specialization becomes much more detailed. It may take the form of a close study of certain stamps, how and why they were produced, how many were printed and sold, and what varieties and errors exist. This usually means researching in old documents and records. The research may only confirm facts already known to other experts, but it may lead to new information or the correction of errors made by earlier authorities on the subject. There are specialised stamp clubs for collectors of this kind which publish bulletins containing interesting articles written by their members. The number of books and articles on philately written in the past fifty years or so runs into thousands, but there is always more to be learned about stamps, postmarks, postal rates and so on.

Concentrating on one country or a group of countries is the commonest form of specialization in stamp collecting (*Figure 17*). But there are many other alternatives. Some collectors restrict themselves to a special kind of stamp, such as Revenue stamps, or

17 Channel Islands stamps: (a) British stamp used in Jersey before 1940; (b) stamp overprinted during the German occupation of Jersey but never used because the islanders protested; (c) 2d stamp bisected and used as a 1d stamp during the war; (d), (e) and (f) wartime issues of Guernsey and Jersey; (g) 1d Channel Islands stamp commemorating the liberation of the islands from German occupation; (h) and (i) Channel Islands regional stamps of the reign of Elizabeth II; (j), (k) and (l) Channel Islands stamps issued after the islands gained independent postal administration in 1969 stamps on a particular topic or theme.

Then there are collectors who specialize in what is called 'postal history'. Collections of this kind often include letters posted in the days before postage stamps came into use, or examples of interesting postmarks.

Postmarks, though much less popular than stamps, can make a very rewarding and varied collection. Some collectors like to collect postmarks with a special historical importance, like 'Gettysburg' (the site of a famous battle in the American Civil War) or 'Guernica' (a Spanish town bombed during the Spanish Civil War and made famous in a painting by Picasso). Others like to collect postmarks with an unusual or amusing name, like 'Sins' (a small town in Switzerland) or 'Seventysix' (Missouri). These days many countries use postal slogans to cancel stamps, telling the public to 'Fight Cancer' or 'Save Fuel', and they can make an interesting collection which may one day have some historical value. Many kinds of special postmark can be found which bear evidence of some special treatment or mistake at the post office, such as the stamped apology, 'Missent to Guyana' on a postcard sent from New York to London.

Certain postmarks may be quite valuable because they are rare; when collecting old used stamps of any country, there are some names which appear in postmarks time and time again while others crop up only once. There was, for example, a village in the West Indies which was destroyed by an earthquake a few months after its post office was opened. Collectors are prepared to pay a lot more for a stamp with rare postmark like that.

Some collectors like to draw a map of the country in which they are interested, marking the location of all the known postmarks. (This is not so large a task as it may appear because not every little post office has its own postmark.) Then they will try to collect an example of each postmark.

Maritime or airmail postmarks are fascinating to some people. They sometimes record a particular exploring expedition, or the maiden voyage of a ship, or the first flight of an aircraft. Occasionally a rather gruesome specimen may turn up, for example a letter which has signs of scorching as the result of an air crash.

Covers (the general word for envelopes, wrappers, etc.) and postmarks of all kinds, like stamps, may often tell a story or form a record of some kind of human activity. One interesting collection consisted of postcards showing mail ships and the places they visited with the *Paquebot* postmarks used on board the ships.

The objects of other collections include postal stationery such as postcards and aerogrammes with the stamp printed or embossed on the paper, or booklets and strips of stamps used in stamp machines in various countries (*Figure 45*). (A stamp from a coiled strip in a stamp machine usually has no perforation at the sides.) The possibilities are endless and the collector can make up his own rules to suit his own interests. Probably he will follow a path trodden by other collectors before, but he may strike out in some new direction, and open up a new branch of philately which no one has studied previously.

6
Obtaining
Stamps

The simplest way of buying stamps is to visit a stamp dealer. He can of course sell individual stamps as well as the packets mentioned earlier. But there are many other ways to purchase stamps. Each collector will find the way which suits him best.

Many stamp dealers send out stamps 'on approval'. They are mounted on sheets of paper or in booklets, and each stamp is marked so the collector can select those he wants. He returns the others together with the money for those he has kept. 'Approvals' are a popular way of buying because the stamps can be examined in the peace and quiet of the collector's home, with no worry about buying a stamp he already has by mistake. Many dealers advertise an approval service in stamp magazines, and sometimes discounts or other special terms are offered. Approvals are a great help when one or two stamps are needed to complete a set.

Some of the major stamp dealers also offer what is called a 'New Issue' service. The collector makes an arrangement for the dealer to send him all the recent issues of a particular country or countries. Usually a deposit has to be paid first. This can be an expensive way to collect, and it is mainly for those who have been collecting for some time and are willing to pay a certain amount of money to keep their collection up to date. However, it is often easier and cheaper than trying to catch up on the new issues at some later time. One other advantage in collecting this way is that whenever a particular new issue is in short supply, a good New Issue dealer will try hard to ensure that his regular customers receive their order. In this way the collector gains, for no trouble and at limited expense, stamps that may well prove quite valuable in the future.

Another way of buying stamps is by studying the advertisements of stamps for sale in stamp magazines and ordering specific sets of individual stamps by mail. When doing this it is essential to have a

Definitives (a) France 3fr; (b) Great Britain 2½d; (c) Angola 1953 20cts (d) Virgin Islands 1938 ½d

Commemoratives (a) Dominica 1976 Bicentenary of American Revolution 2 cents; (b) Republic of Malagasy, Bicentenary of American Revolution 40fr

Revenue stamps (a) Montserrat 1880 1d; (b) St Vincent 1883 5 shillings; (c) Northern Rhodesia 1953 6d

Stephenson's Locomotion
7ᴾ
1825 Stockton and Darlington Railway

BELIZE
EↃR
Internal Mail Service 1910
45c   Centenary of UPU Membership 1879–1979

3ʳ·   MALAWI
DIESEL RAIL CAR

POLSKA   1 ⅝ᵲ
PKP ET22-001
Uniwersalna lokomotywa elektryczna ET-22·1969

JERSEY   GOREY
"CAESAREA"   AUGUST 6th 1873
St HELIER   9ᴾ
Centenary·Inauguration of Jersey Eastern Railway
G. DRUMMOND   COURVOISIER S.A.

RHODESIA   1/6
GARRATT CLASS 15A 1950
BEIRA-SALISBURY 1899

نيل جوي
٣
ريال
AIRMAIL
3
RIYALS
J.M.S.
AJMAN STATE
AND ITS DEPENDENCIES

1873 – 1973
Steam Railway Centenary
Kissack 2-4-0
ISLE of MAN   7½p
J H NICHOLSON B.I.   1973   HARRISON & SONS LTD

125th ANNIVERSARY of the RAILWAY
THE PROJECTOR – 1845
JAMAICA   3c

WHITCOMB LOCOMOTIVE 65 H.P. 1949   20c
MAURITIUS

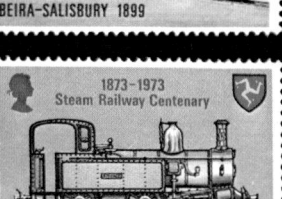

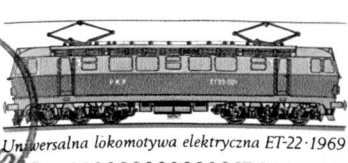

Thematic stamps from many countries showing (a) railway engines (b) flowers

Provisionals with surcharges (a) Dominica ½d on 1d; (b) Seychelles 1903 3 cents on 45 cents; King Edward VII surcharged locally in Victoria, Seychelles; (c) Sarawak 1892 1 cent on 3 cents, surcharge Sir Charles Brooke; (d) Sierra Leone 1965 3 cents on 1d, surcharged in Freetown, Sierra Leone

Overprinted for use in another country (a) Leeward Islands 6d overprinted Barbuda; (b) British ½d overprinted Zululand; (c) Bermuda ½d overprinted Gibraltar; (d) Seychelles 1968 2 rupees 25 cents overprinted B.I.O.T. (British Indian Ocean Territory)

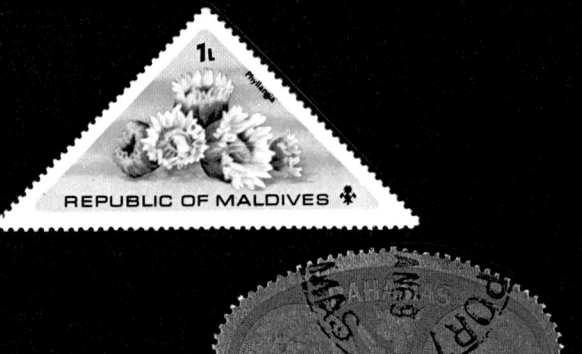 

Some odd shapes

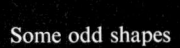

catalogue handy to make sure you are quite clear what you are buying, and it is worth comparing different advertisements to make certain of getting the best bargain.

Though not really intended for young or inexperienced collectors, auctions are an increasingly popular way of buying and selling stamps. Some auctions are held in public, with the bidders gathered in one room. Others are conducted entirely by mail: each customer writes down the maximum he is willing to pay for any lot in the auction, and the highest bid wins. It is also possible to make bids by post in public auctions. The auctioneers publish a catalogue containing descriptions of each lot for sale; a single lot may be an individual stamp or it may be a whole collection. Most auction catalogues also contain an estimate of the selling prices or a reserve figure for each lot which must be reached before the lot can be sold. Sometimes a lot can be bought for less than the estimate, but sometimes it fetches much more.

There is no reason why a young collector should not buy stamps through an auction provided he takes advice from a more experienced collector and sets himself strict rules. He should decide in advance what a particular lot is worth to him and how much he can afford to pay for it. Then, on no account should he go higher than that figure. Sometimes, when two or more people want a particular lot in a public auction, the price can rise unexpectedly and very fast. It is easy to get carried away and end by paying a lot more than necessary. Remember, there is nearly always another way of buying that stamp anyway.

A popular and inexpensive way of expanding a collection is to swap or exchange stamps with other collectors. The other collector may not collect the stamps of all the countries you want, but this may be an advantage, for he may well have unwanted stamps that are of interest to you. Other collectors will probably be met at school or college or elsewhere. An even better way to get to know other collectors is by joining a stamp club. Stamp clubs vary in size, and while some are composed of general collectors, others cater for more specialized interests. There are many of them. There is probably one in your home town, and if not, perhaps you are the person to start one.

Before swapping any stamps, it is just as well to make sure you know their value. (When collectors talk about the 'value' of a stamp they mean the price listed in one of the well-known catalogues such as Stanley Gibbons in Great Britain or Scotts in the United States.) Two stamps of equal value according to the catalogue may be exchanged directly, but as a rule things are more complicated. In a stamp club, the commonest way of exchanging stamps is through booklets or approvals made up by the individual members. These booklets are placed in a club box and the members choose those they need. They pay the money for the stamps they take to the club organizer, who also pays them any money owing from sales of their own stamps. In this way collectors can circulate their swaps and fill gaps in their collections at very little cost (prices are much lower than catalogue values), or at a profit if their own duplicates have sold well.

Stamps can also be swapped by post. A collector who specialises in (for example) the stamps of Canada, may be able to find a pen friend in Canada who specializes in the stamps of his own country. This kind of contact is very useful to both of them. Some foreign embassies may be willing to help find a pen friend in their countries. Some stamp magazines print the names and addresses of collectors looking for a pen friend.

7
Different Kinds
of Stamps

Something the new collector soon discovers is that not all stamps are used for the pre-payment of postage. The first packet of mixed stamps he buys may contain a few examples of stamps produced for another purpose. They include Postage Due stamps, Revenue stamps and other kinds which may be found on letters, as well as stamps having nothing to do with postage, such as trading stamps or gift stamps. The main types are described below. All these stamps may of course be collected; but it is important to make a clear division between postage stamps and non-postage stamps.

Adhesive postage stamps are themselves divided into a number of distinct categories, and in stamp catalogues they are frequently listed under these categories. The standard issues of each country, the commonest types of postage stamp, are called *definitive* stamps (*Figure 18*). These are produced for everyday postal use, usually over a long period of time. Sets of definitives are generally quite large as they have to include values for the whole scale of postal charges. In most countries definitives are comparatively small - roughly the classic size of the Penny Black - and have a simple design such as the head of the ruler.

The early stamps of all countries were definitives. It was not until the late 1880s that someone had the idea of *commemorative* stamps - stamps issued to mark an anniversary or a special event or to honour a certain person (*Figure 19*). As a rule, commemoratives have exactly the same purpose as definitives, but they are normally in use for a short time only, and sets are often quite small -sometimes only a single stamp. They are usually large, pictorial stamps. It is difficult to say which country issued the first com-memoratives. The United States issued a series of stamps in 1892 to

mark the 400th anniversary of the discovery of the New World by
Christopher Columbus. Other early commemoratives celebrated the
500th anniversary of Prince Henry the Navigator (Portugal, 1894)
and the first modern Olympic Games (Greece, 1896).

In the present century commemoratives have become very common, partly because governments have discovered that stamps can
be a useful source of income. Stamps are bought by stamp collectors as well as by people wishing to use them on letters, so that even
stamps which have no practical purpose can be sold in large
numbers - to collectors. Hence the ever-growing number of commemorative issues which roll off the printing presses every few
months in nearly every country of the world. These stamps are not
designed primarily for normal postal purposes, for which the
definitive issues are perfectly adequate. They are really a form of
national publicity, calling attention to some person or event connected with the country issuing the stamp. However, there is
another reason for issuing commemoratives: they can be sold to
stamp collectors. In a small country the sale of postage stamps is
often a large source of government income: in some little countries
stamps are the main export. Governments are therefore tempted to
issue more and more stamps in the knowledge that collectors
around the world will buy them.

Many philatelists feel that this is an unfortunate development.
Some countries have a reputation for shamelessly exploiting stamp
collectors by issuing vast quantities of commemoratives, very few (if
any) of which are used as ordinary postage stamps. However, it is
hard to see why the governments of those countries should be
blamed. As long as collectors keep buying their stamps, they will no
doubt go on producing more issues. It is a less painful way of
raising money than (for example) increasing taxes.

In recent years a new category of pictorial stamps has appeared.
Often called *thematic* or *topical* stamps, they too are aimed at the
collector. They show a series of pictorial subjects on common
themes, such as birds, animals, fish, boats, etc. Dealers and collectors usually treat thematic stamps as a form of commemorative,
though they do not necessarily 'commemorate' anything. Many
collectors specialise in thematics, basing their collection on such
themes as 'transport' or 'nature'. One famous private collection made

18 Some definitive stamps from (a) Mozambique; (b) United States; (c) Gold Coast; (d) North Borneo

19 (a) A set of commemorative stamps from Trinidad and Tobago

19 (b) A set of commemorative stamps from St Christopher-Nevis-Anguilla

19 (c) A set of stamps from Barbados issued to commemorate the diamond jubilee of the Girl Guides

by a doctor contained stamps from all over the world on the theme of 'medicine'.

A number of countries have started to produce *miniature* or *souvenir sheets*, usually as part of some commemorative or thematic issue (*Figure 20*). They are printed sheets with one (or more) of the stamps in the set surrounded by some kind of ornamental design or inscription. These sheets are gummed, and the stamp(s) - or the whole sheet if you have a big enough envelope - can be used in the same way as ordinary stamps. Sometimes the stamps featured in miniature sheets have variations in watermark or perforation. They are eagerly pursued by certain specialist collectors, but they are obviously aimed at the stamp collector rather than the citizen with a letter to post. For that reason, many collectors prefer to avoid them.

It sometimes happens that a country runs out of the right kind of postage stamps as a result of a change in the currency, or through an unexpected shortage of a stamp of a particular denomination, or postal value. If that happens, *provisional* stamps may be issued until the proper stamps can be reprinted. The most famous provisional stamp, printed locally, was the British Guiana 1 cent of 1856, the world's rarest stamp. Not all provisional stamps, however, are particularly valuable.

A common type of provisional stamp consists of a normal stampwith a new denomination or *surcharge* overprinted on it. In the nineteenth century many countries had their stamps printed elsewhere. The stamps of many British colonies, like British Guiana, were printed in England (the stamps of St Helena in the Atlantic Ocean and St Vincent in the Caribbean still are). Occasionally, the local post office would run out of stamps of a certain denomination before the new supply arrived by ship from England. Another denomination would then be overprinted on a stamp that was not in short supply. For example, if it happened that there were no 2 pence but plenty of 1 penny stamps, some of the 1 pennies would be overprinted to act as 2 pence stamps. A local printer would do the overprinting, and errors were not uncommon. Such errors are eagerly hunted by collectors today. Sometimes stamps are bisected and only half used on the envelope. One example is the ½ penny on 6 pence St Vincent error (*Figure 36*).

20 Miniature sheets from (a) Montserrat (soldiers of British regiments) and (b) the Cayman Islands (advertising tourism)

The collector soon learns that some stamps can be difficult to identify. Many provisional issues fall into this category. One type of provisional stamp that turns up occasionally is a stamp of one country overprinted with the name of another. When the Caribbean island of Montserrat asked the British Government for its own stamps in 1876, it was decided that this would be too expensive, and instead the stamps of neighbouring Antigua were used with 'Montserrat' overprinted. And when postage stamps were introduced in Gibraltar in 1886, the first issue consisted of seven stamps of the Atlantic island of Bermuda, overprinted 'Gibraltar'. These overprinted stamps were replaced by the first Gibraltar stamps later in the same year and are now quite rare.

In the past, a number of countries issued special stamps for mail travelling by air (*Figure 21*). Airmail stamps are usually easy to recognise by their design, which often includes an aeroplane and the word 'airmail'. They were very popular in the 1930s, when commercial air routes were being opened for the first time. Today they are less common, as most countries use the same stamps for air and surface mail. A letter going by air is more often indicated either by a sticky blue label or a striped border in bright colours on the envelope.

In many countries it is possible to send mail extra-fast by *Express* or *Special Delivery*, when the letter is delivered by a special messenger. Some countries, notably the United States, have issued stamps for these services which, of course, are more expensive than the ordinary post.

21 Airmail stamps from the United States and St Lucia

Some countries have special envelopes, wrappers or postcards with the stamp already printed or impressed on the paper. This *postal stationery* is in a separate category: it does not have the adhesive back which is one of the accepted characteristics of postage stamps, and therefore it is ignored by most stamp collectors. However, there is no reason why a person should not collect postal stationery as well as, or instead of, stamps, and some people do specialise in this interesting sideline.

Most collectors restrict themselves to collecting genuine postage stamps and reject not only postal stationery but all stamps produced for other, non-postal purposes. This may seem a quite simple decision to make, but in fact it is not always so straightforward, and one often finds stamps used for non-postal purposes appearing in both general and specialised collections. They may be interlopers which have crept in among their postal cousins by mistake. But often they have been included deliberately by the collector, because they seemed attractive or interesting and added a touch of variety.

Most people are familiar with *Postage Due* stamps. Strictly speaking, they are classified as postage stamps though they are not used for prepayment of postage. If a letter is sent through the mail with no stamps on it, or with stamps of a value less than the charge due, then the Post Office makes an extra charge which is paid by the person receiving the letter. The Post Office sticks Postage Due stamps on the letter which indicate the amount that has to be paid (it is usually double the cost of prepaid postage.) These stamps are not for sale to the public as a rule, but certain post offices, which specialize in service for philatelists, will sell mint (unused) Postage Due stamps to collectors. That is the only way of obtaining unused examples, as the Postage Due stamps on a letter are always franked by the post office (*Figure 22*).

22 Postage due stamps: a modern one from Great Britain and a locally printed one from St Lucia, 1931

Another close cousin of the postage stamp is the *Revenue* or *Fiscal* stamp. Postage stamps have other uses as well as the normal one of acting as a receipt for prepayment of postage. They may be used to pay some kind of tax. Stamp duty is an obvious example, and in Britain until quite recently the signature on a receipt was usually written across a 2 pence stamp.

Nowadays, most countries use the same issue for both postage and revenue. That is why many stamps bear the words 'Postage and Revenue' or their equivalent in another language. An early stamp of this kind was the 1 penny lilac of Great Britain, issued in 1881 with the inscription 'Postage and Inland Revenue'.

At that time, however, it was the general rule to produce stamps separately for postal and revenue purposes. These revenue stamps often turn up in old collections. As both postage and revenue stamps were often printed by the same firm, stamps intended for revenue use were frequently identical with the postage stamps except for the overprinted word 'Revenue'. Sometimes a collector may come across a revenue stamp which bears a postmark, proving that it was actually used as a postage - not revenue - stamp. Such stamps are known as 'postal-fiscals', but beware: many of these stamps are fakes.

Another sub-group of stamps used in some countries during the 19th century are *Telegraph* stamps (*Figure 23*). As you might guess they were intended to be used for paying telegraph or telegram charges but, like revenue stamps, they were occasionally authorized for postal use also. In that case they are known as 'postal-telegraphs'. Nowadays, when stamps are employed in connection with telegrams, the ordinary postage stamps of the country are used.

There are many other categories of stamps which the collector is likely to come across sooner or later. During the First World War,

23 Telegraph stamp from Western Australia, 1886

24 Stamps surcharged to raise money for war tax (a) and (b), and for charity (c)

25 Stamps overprinted to show they are for use on official mail

War Tax stamps were issued in some British colonies which bore a surcharge to raise money to pay for the war. *Charity* stamps are a better-known example of this method of raising money. They bear a surcharge which is devoted to a particular charity. One example issued in Britain in 1975 showed an invalid in a wheelchair and the values 4½ pence and 1½ pence. The first is the postal denomination of the stamp and the second figure is the surcharge for charity (*Figure 24*).

Special stamps have sometimes been printed to be used on the mail sent out by government departments. Often, these *Official* stamps are the ordinary definitives of the country with 'Official',

26 Special categories: (a) New Zealand health stamp, (b) U.S. parcel post, (c) Austrian newspaper stamp, (d) Dominican Republic stamp for presidential mail, (e) Czechoslovak personal delivery stamp

'Service', 'OHMS' (in Britain, standing for 'On Her Majesty's Service') or some such word overprinted (*Figure 25*). Stamp collectors usually collect them in the same way as ordinary stamps.

Other categories of stamps which have been issued at various times include health stamps, parcel stamps, registration stamps newspaper stamps and railway stamps. It is not always easy to decide whether these special categories fall within the boundaries of general stamp collecting or not. As a rough guide, they can usually be classed among the family of postage stamps when the government that issued them authorized their general public use (*Figure 26 a, b* and *c*). Stamps or sticky labels that do not belong within the family are sometimes called *Cinderella* stamps.

The endless variety of stamps can be illustrated by two examples of stamps issued for special purposes. A 25 cents stamp of the Dominican Republic was issued in 1935 bearing a picture of the presidential palace. This stamp had to be stuck on any letter addressed to the president of the republic. In 1937 and again in 1946 Czechoslovakia issued its 'Personal Delivery' stamps. They ensured a remarkable postal service. Any letter bearing one of these triangular stamps was delivered directly into the hands of the person to whom it was addressed, and to no one else (*Figure 26d,e*).

8
Identifying
Stamps

When sorting out the stamps in a packet bought in a store or in a collection given by a friend or relative, the newcomer to collecting will probably come across some difficult problems. The first one is simply to decide what country each stamp comes from.

A large number of the stamps will have the name of the country and other information (such as the postal value) in English. Stamps of Commonwealth countries, for example, nearly always carry the name of their country in English, although some include the name in another language as well. The names of many other countries, although in a different language, are still sufficiently similar to their English equivalents for most collectors to guess what they are. It does not take an expert linguist to realise that *Belgique* is Belgium, *Island* is Iceland and *Norge* is Norway, or that *Française* and *Italiane* must be connected with France and Italy. Other foreign names have to be learned, but there are not too many of them and collectors soon grow familiar with them even if they do not speak any other language themselves. After seeing the name on a few stamps, it is easy to remember that *Helvetia* is Switzerland, *Magyar* is Hungary, *Österreich* is Austria, etc.,

But when these stamps have been sorted out, the collector will still be left with a number which have not yet been identified. Some will not carry a country's name at all, only the word 'postage' and a figure to show the postal value. These may well be British stamps, which never show the name of the country (although they do always show the head of the reigning monarch). The first stamps of Brazil, which were nicknamed 'Bull's Eyes' because of the shape of their design (*Figure 27*), were also issued without an inscription from 1843 until 1866. Today however, stamps without the name of the issuing country are very unusual, and the new collector will seldom come across any except British. These unnamed stamps,

27 A Brazilian
'Bull's Eye' of about
1860

28 Two stamps from Thailand, formerly
called Siam, giving the name of the country
in English as well as in the native alphabet

which are sometimes called *mute* stamps, are not, therefore, a
serious problem.

Certain countries with rather long names do not print their full
names on their stamps but use an abbreviation. Some common examples are 'U.S.' for United States (of America), 'C.C.C.P.' for
the Union of Soviet Socialist Republics (Soviet Russia), 'R.S.A.'
for Republic of South Africa and 'U.A.R.' for United Arab
Republic (Egypt). These too are easily remembered.

A more serious difficulty arises with countries which have not
only a different language but also a different alphabet, such as
China and the Arab countries. The collector will find the task of
identifying these stamps easier if he has a general idea of what
Chinese, Arabic and other forms of writing look like (they are very
distinctive). This will point him in the right direction, but he still
may have to track down the actual countries concerned. The
simplest way of doing this is to flip through the pages of a well-
illustrated stamp catalogue looking for pictures of stamps bearing
the name or words that have to be identified.

The commonest unfamiliar alphabets are Arabic (spoken in most
countries of the Middle East), Chinese, Greek and Russian. They
may, however, crop up in unexpected places. For instance, some
early Polish issues were printed in Russian because Poland was then
under Russian rule. Among other countries using different
alphabets which the collector will have to identify are Thailand

(Siam), Iran (Persia), Mongolia, Tibet and India. Some modern issues give the name of the country in English as well as in the native language (*Figure 28*). This can be a great help in identifying earlier issues on which the English name does not appear.

But it is not enough to know the present name of every stamp-issuing country. During the past century or so since postage stamps came into general use throughout the world, some new independent countries have emerged and some have disappeared. A much greater number have changed their name. Many African countries, for example, changed their name when they ceased to be colonies and became fully independent states. Collectors of Commonwealth stamps will soon become familiar with the names of former British colonies in Africa, such as the Gold Coast (now Ghana), Northern Rhodesia (now Zambia), Nyasaland (now Malawi) and several more. Malawi is a good example. Those who collect the stamps of this African state know that it was once 'Nyasaland', but at an earlier period it was part of 'British Central Africa', and for a short time its stamps were inscribed 'Rhodesia and Nyasaland'.

The same kind of problems occur with the French-speaking countries of Africa, many of which formerly belonged to French West Africa or French Equatorial Africa. Gabon, for example, had its own stamps in the 1880s; from 1889 to 1904 it used the stamps of the French Congo; from 1904 to 1937 it was again a separate colony with its own stamps; in 1937 it changed to the stamps of French Equatorial Africa; finally, in 1960, it became the independent republic of Gabon with, of course, a new type of stamp yet again.

When all the stamps have been sorted into their correct countries, the first process of identification is complete. New collectors may feel that it is enough for the time being, but soon they will want to go further, and divide the stamps of each country into sets. This is usually quite easy as all the stamps in a set tend to look alike (although, as always, there are some exceptions). The question then arises: is the set complete, and if not, what stamps are missing? These questions can only be answered with the help of a stamp catalogue.

Catalogues
A stamp catalogue is basically the price list of a dealer. However, over the years it has developed into an invaluable reference book.

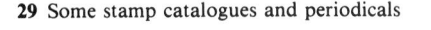

29 Some stamp catalogues and periodicals

Major catalogues list, country by country, every authentic postage stamp ever issued, with its date, its price or value (used and unused), and a number of other details concerning colour variations, watermarks, perforations and so on.

Stamp catalogues are published by several firms. Among the best-known and most reliable are Stanley Gibbons in Britain and Scott in the United States. Excellent catalogues are also produced in other languages, notably Yvert et Tellier (French) and Zumstein (German) (*Figure 29*).

Besides their large general catalogues, firms like Stanley Gibbons also publish more specialised catalogues on individual countries or groups of countries, and sometimes - these are for the really advanced collector - even on individual issues. The main catalogues are published in new editions every year.

A good catalogue is expensive, but no collector can progress very far without one. It is possible to borrow one from a public library, but for young collectors with not much money to spend the best plan is to buy a second-hand catalogue. They are much less expensive than new editions and although, being second-hand, they will be slightly out of date, that does not matter very much to the collector who needs a catalogue to help him identify his stamps. (If he wants to know the latest prices, he can consult a more recent edition of the catalogue in the library.)

At first glance the catalogue may seem very complicated, but once the system is understood, it is no more difficult to use than a dictionary. All stamp catalogues are laid out in much the same way, and once you have mastered one you have mastered them all. The stamps of each country are listed in chronological order, starting with the first issue and going right up to the present. One minor exception to this rule concerns later additions to a set of definitives. It sometimes happens that a country finds it necessary to issue new values in its standard definitive set to cater for an increase in postal charges or for some other reason. In the catalogue, all the stamps belonging to the set are listed together, even if some individual stamps were issued at a later date. The lowest face value appears at the top of the list and the highest at the bottom. Specialised stamps such as Postage Dues or Airmails are sometimes listed separately at the end of each country.

A section of a page from one of the catalogues produced by Stanley Gibbons is reproduced on page 68. It shows how much useful information the catalogue provides for each stamp or set: the date the stamps were issued, their values, their colours or shades, details of the printer and printing process and, if known, the name of the designer. It also describes the type of watermark and the size of the perforation. The two columns of figures give valuations for mint stamps (on the left) and for used stamps (on the right) (*Figure 30*).

A word of warning about valuations: the figures given in the catalogue are not necessarily the market price, and a stamp valued at £100 in the catalogue may actualy be worth far less. It all depends on its condition. The catalogue valuation is for a stamp in

BRITISH GUIANA   193

56. Botanical Gardens.

57. Victoria Regia Lilies.

58. Amerindian
shooting Fish.

60. Rice Combine-harvester.

62. Felling
Greenheart.

63. Mining for Bauxite.

64. Mount Roraima.

66. Arapaima.

(Centre litho., frame recess ($1); recess (others).
Waterlow (until 1961), then D.L.R.)

1954 (1 Dec.)–**62.** *Wmk. Mult. Script CA.*
P 12½ × 13* (*horiz.*) or 13 (*vert.*).

331	**55**	1 c. black	5	5
332	**56**	2 c. myrtle-green ..	8	5
333	**57**	3 c. brn.-olive & red-brn.	8	5
334	**58**	4 c. violet..	8	5
		a. D.L.R.ptg.(*shades*)(5.12.61)	20	20
335	**59**	5 c. scarlet and black ..	8	8
336	**60**	6 c. yellow-green (*shades*)	8	8
337	**61**	8 c. ultramarine (*shades*)	8	10
338	**62**	12 c. black and reddish brown (*shades*) ..	35	30
339	**63**	24 c. black and brownish orange (*shades*) ..	35	30
340	**64**	36 c. rose-carmine & black	35	25
341	**65**	48 c. ultramarine & brown-lake (*shades*).. ..	45	40
		ab. D.L.R. ptg. *Brt. ultram. & pale brown-lake* (19.9.61)	1·50	1·75
342	**66**	72 c. carmine & emerald ..	75	75
		a. D.L.R. ptg. (17.7.62) ..	1·75	2·00
343	**67**	$1 pink, yell., grn. & blk.	85	50
344	**68**	$2 deep mauve (*shades*)	1·75	1·10
345	**69**	$5 ultramarine & black	4·00	4·25
		a. D.L.R. ptg. (19.9.61) ..	7·00	8·00
331/345*a*		.. .. *Set of* 15	8·50	7·50

The separately listed De La Rue printings are
identifiable as singles by the single wide-tooth
perfs. at each side at the *bottom* of the stamps. In
the Waterlow these wide teeth are at the *top*.
*All the Waterlow printings and early De La
Rue printings of the horizontal designs measure
12.3 × 12.8, but De La Rue printings of 22nd
May, 1962 and all later printings (including
those on the Block CA watermark), measure
12.3 × 12.6.

II. SELF-GOVERNMENT.

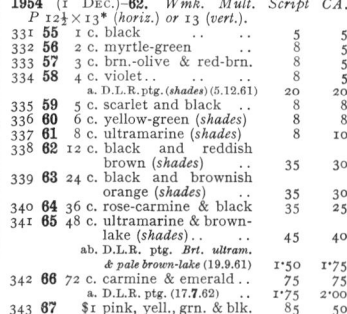

70

(Photo. Harrison.)

1961 (23 Oct.). *History and Culture Week.*
W w.**12.** *P* 14½ × 14.

346	**70**	5 c. sepia and orange-red	10	12
347	,,	6 c. sepia and blue-green	12	12
348	,,	30 c. sepia & yellow-orange	35	40

1963 (14 July). *Freedom from Hunger. As No.
76 of Aden.*

349	20 c. reddish violet	30	30

1963 (2 Sept.). *Red Cross Centenary. As Nos.
147/8 of Antigua.*

350	5 c. red and black	12	12
351	20 c. red and blue	45	50

1963–65. *As Nos.* 333/44, *but wmk.* w.**12.**

354	**57**	3 c. brown-olive and red-brown (12.65) ..	30	35
356	**59**	5 c. scarlet & blk. (28.5.64)	10	5
359	**62**	12 c. black and yellowish		

30 Part of a page from a stamp catalogue

good condition. On a used stamp, for example, the postmark should be clear and neat. Stamps that are torn or have a heavily smudged postmark may be worth little or nothing, whatever the valuation in the catalogue. Unfortunately, many old stamps are faded, or marked with rusty spots (called foxing), or have some other fault. In some old collections the stamps were glued down on the page. Others may have damaged edges due to careless cutting from an imperforate sheet, or rubbed-off corners, or stained surfaces. These defects will seriously reduce their value. That high-priced stamp in your grandfather's collection has to be a good specimen if it is to be worth as much as the catalogue says it is. It is possible for a really outstanding specimen to be worth even more, but the chances are that it will be worth less.

When sorting out duplicates to be exchanged, it is worth making sure that the two (or more) duplicates really are copies of exactly the same stamp. Although they appear identical at first glance, a close examination may reveal slight differences. Sometimes different kinds of paper were used for different printings. Sometimes the watermark or the perforation was changed. It may be that two 'twins' are in fact different stamps. The catalogue will describe these small variations between printings, and by careful study the collector can find out exactly what variations of a particular stamp he owns, and what others may exist.

Watermarks

A watermark is a design.or pattern impressed in the paper, not printed on its surface. During the manufacture of the paper, the soft paper pulp is pressed by a moving cylinder. The cylinder carries the watermark pattern made in wire, and where the wire is pressed in by the cylinder the paper is made very slightly thinner. Some ordinary writing paper has a watermark (usually giving the name or trademark of the maker) which can be seen when the paper is held up to the light. Nearly all banknotes have watermarks, and so do postage stamps. The reason is the same in both cases - to make them more difficult to forge.

It is fairly easy to see the watermark in a banknote but less easy in a stamp. Sometimes the watermark is extremely faint and barely visible to the naked eye. A magnifying glass may help. A simple method of recognising watermarks which is used by many collec-

tors is to place the stamp face down on a smooth black surface.
Dealers sell little trays for this purpose but any flat piece of black
plastic or tile is equally good. A few drops of benzine are dropped
on to the back of the stamp, which makes the watermark show up
more clearly. However, the collector should be cautious when using
benzine or any other chemical on stamps. If the stamps contain certain dyes or are printed on chalk paper, the colours may run or the
paper may be damaged.

When sheets of paper pass through the printing press to be
printed as sheets of stamps, the watermark will normally appear in
the same place in each stamp. Sometimes, however, a sheet may be
passed through sideways or the wrong way round. When that happens, the printed stamps will be exactly the same as on any other
sheet, but the watermark will appear sideways or upside down ('inverted'). Supposing that happens just once or twice during the prin-

31 Watermarks: (a) Large Star in stamps printed by Perkins, Bacon; (b) Crown over
CC ('Crown Colonies') in stamps printed by De La Rue; (c) Crown over CA ('Crown
Agents') on stamps printed by De La Rue; (d) Multiple Crown CA, 1904; (e) Multiple
Script CA. 1921; (f) Multiple PTM, introduced in Malayan issues, 1961; (g) Multiple
Crown CA Diagonal, introduced for Churchill centenary stamps, 1964; (h) Water-
mark found in stamps of the Australian states, around 1900

ting, a small number of stamps out of the whole issue will have a sideways or inverted watermark. That makes them rare and, of course, valuable.

With definitive sets which go on being reprinted for many years, a new type of watermark is sometimes introduced although the printed design of the stamps themselves is not altered. The new watermark nevertheless makes them different. With help from the catalogue, such stamps can be sorted into different sets according to their watermarks (*Figure 31*).

Perforations

Nowadays, sheets of postage stamps are made with lines of little holes, called perforations, which make it easier to detach a stamp from the sheet. But the earliest stamps were issued on plain sheets of paper and had to be separated with scissors or a knife. These stamps are known as 'imperforate'.

When selecting an imperforate stamp for the collection, the collector should make sure that a good margin exists beyond the edges of the printed stamp design. It is not unknown for a cunning and unscrupulous person to trim the edges of a more modern, perforated stamp to make it look like an imperforate.

The man who is usually given the credit for inventing the neat idea of perforations was an Irishman named Henry Archer. The first technique to assist in separating stamps from the sheet was called *rouletting*. A wheel with little spikes around its rim was run down the lines between the stamps making small slits in the paper. The slits were sometimes straight and sometimes curved.

Unlike rouletting, which simply makes cuts without removing any actual paper from the sheet, perforating machines punch out lines of small holes. There are two main types of perforation, *line* perforation and *comb* perforation, which is the type most often used today. Line perforation is made by a machine which punches a single row of holes at a time. First it makes them up and down the sheet, then across. Inevitably, the two lines of holes do not match perfectly at each corner of the stamps. The corners of line-perforated stamps therefore usually appear slightly irregular. In comb perforation, the lines of holes are made in both directions at the same time, and the result is that the holes at the corners of the stamps coincide exactly, giving a neater appearance. The difference

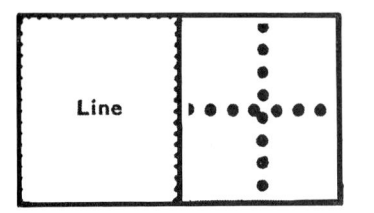
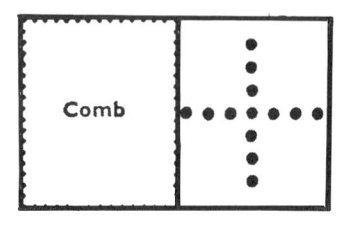

32 Perforations (a) Line   (b) Comb

between line and comb perforation is most easily seen in a block of four (or more) stamps (*Figure 32*).

Perforations vary a good deal. They are measured by the number of holes in a space of 2 cm, and most catalogues record the number of perforations in that space to the nearest half or quarter. If there are twelve holes in a 2-cm space, the catalogue will say 'Perf. 12'. However, sometimes the perforation in lines going across the sheet (i.e. at the top and bottom of each stamp) is different from the lines going up and down (at the sides of each stamp). If the catalogue says, for example, 'Perf. 12 x 13', this means that the perforation at top and bottom is 12 holes in 2 cm and the perforation at the sides is 13 holes in 2 cm.

Perforations can be measured with special gauges, which are sold with instructions on their use. After a little practice, the collector will find his perforation gauge a simple and useful tool. There is an illustration of a perforation gauge on page 84.

9
Stamp
Albums

Choosing an album to house a stamp collection is a matter of personal taste, like choosing a new shirt or dress. There are many types available and each collector must decide how much he or she can afford to spend and which album is most suitable for the collection.

There are two main types: those with printed names of countries (and other details) at the head of the page, and those with no printed words in which the collector himself writes the details on each page.

The simplest kind of printed album is usually provided in the stamp collector's outfit that many people buy when they begin collecting. At the top of each page is the name of the country, sometimes with a few useful facts and pictures of that country's stamps. The rest of the page is divided into squares by dotted lines, which assist in mounting the stamps in straight lines. Stamps these days come in all shapes and sizes, and they will not all fit into the dotted squares. An album of this kind is fine for a general collection of a thousand or so stamps, but as the collection grows the stamps will overflow the space provided for them. Most young collectors soon find they need a bigger album, and a collector who starts off with a large number of stamps might consider missing out this stage altogether by buying a larger album or one that gives room for growth.

At this second stage, there are several alternatives available. For most collectors, the choice will probably be some kind of loose-leaf album. A common type has a spring-back cover, which allows sheets to be inserted or removed. Each sheet is printed with the name of a country on one side only. Albums of this type are especially useful for the general collector who is not interested in specialization. Extra pages can be added for a particular country when they are needed, and empty pages can be removed. New pages

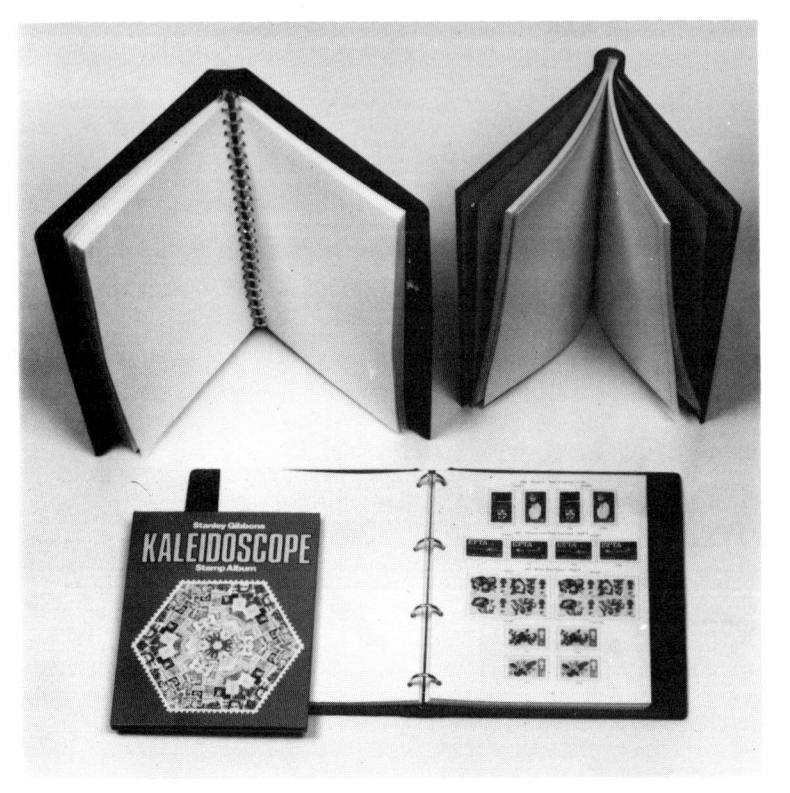

33 Stamp albums

can be obtained and added to the album, and it is a good idea to buy some extra pages when buying the album (*Figure 33*).

A more advanced type of printed album has a space specially printed for each stamp, a very tidy arrangement. One hundred years ago it would have been possible to buy an album containing a space for each stamp issued by every country in the world. That is hardly possible now. It would require a whole bookcase of albums, even if any one collector had the time and money for such a collection. Today, albums of this type are made only for specialised collections. There is one for all the stamps of the United States, another for all the Commonwealth stamps of the reign of George VI, and many more. Albums of this type are becoming increasingly popular. New pages are published for new issues, although there is often a long gap between the new issue of stamps and the publication of the pages designed for them,

These albums are not suitable for every kind of collection. Many collectors like to 'write up' their own collection, or they wish to include the odd cover (envelope, wrapper, postcard, etc.), variety or special postmark for which there is no printed space. They prefer a plain, loose-leaf album which has no printing at all except for a pale network of small squares, like graph paper, which helps in mounting and arranging the stamps neatly. Any necessary facts are written in by hand.

This is the most versatile type of stamp album, and there is a a vast variety to choose from. Some are quite inexpensive. Others, with pages of stiff card and leather binding, are rather costly. The great advantage of the loose-leaf album is that major changes can be made in the arrangement of the collection quite easily. To begin with, there may be several countries sharing one album. As the numbers grow, some countries can be moved out to another album of the same type. Even if the collector's special interest changes, it is not necessary to start all over again with a new album.

Album leaves, or pages, are usually printed on white paper, but in recent years some have appeared with black paper. Most stamps look better against a black background, but one slight drawback of black paper is that writing up the collection has to be done in white pencil or ink.

Loose-leaf albums may have spring-back covers, or the pages may be pierced to be held by a ring binder or some similar system. Spring binders are more difficult to open out flat than ring binders, but ring binders tend to tear the page at the holes unless handled with care. It is a matter of personal choice, but one point to bear in mind is that stamp albums must usually withstand more wear and tear than ordinary books. They should be strongly made, to protect the collection as well as to display it. It is therefore unwise to buy an album in haste. The best plan is to visit a stamp dealer who has a large stock, and consider very carefully which one is most suitable before making a decision. If the album chosen is too expensive, it may be better to wait until you can afford it than to make do with a cheap substitute.

Finally, remember that stamp collections grow, and try to make allowances for that. For the same reason, if there is any suspicion

that a particular album may go out of print, it should be avoided as
spare pages will become unobtainable.

It is also possible to buy albums for collections which do not con-
sist of postage stamps only. Some people like to collect complete
covers, often 'First Day of Issue' covers. Specialised albums for
these and other types of collection can be obtained, and the same
rules apply: study the albums available and allow for the growth of
the collection. It is worth remembering that there is always a
market for 'second-hand' stamps, but there is very little demand
for second hand albums!

10
Preparing and Arranging a Collection

Some stamp collectors prefer to concentrate on either mint or used stamps, but most people collect both kinds. Before used stamps can be placed in the album it is often necessary to remove bits of paper or old stamp hinges from the back. This should be done carefully to avoid damaging the stamp. The most common method is to float the stamps, face up, in a saucer or shallow bowl of clean water. The paper gradually absorbs moisture, and after a few minutes it can be peeled cleanly from the stamp.

'Floating off' stamps in this way requires some patience. It is tempting to hurry the process by removing the stamp too soon and perhaps tearing it as a result. When the stamp is taken from the water, it should be turned face down and the surplus paper peeled very gently away from the stamp (not the other way round). If any resistance is felt then the paper is not yet soaked through, and the stamp needs to float on the water a little longer.

Another danger which has to be avoided when separating stamps from paper occurs when there is ink on the paper close to the stamp, probably from the address written on the envelope. Ink from a fountain pen will run when it gets wet, and may stain the stamp. The answer is to cut carefully around the stamp, removing all paper with writing on it.

There are other methods of removing paper from used stamps. Some collectors, for example, use a flat box containing several layers of wet blotting paper. The important point is not to try removing the stamp without first damping the paper in some way, even if it seems to be attached quite loosely. Not only is that likely to cause damage, it may leave some surplus gum on the stamp which will stick to the page of the album or, even worse, to other stamps.

When the paper has been removed, the stamp should be placed

face down on a piece of dry, unused blotting paper and left there until it is completely dry. It is best to let it dry naturally. Placing it on a radiator or running an iron over it will certainly speed things up but may damage the stamp. If a stamp curls while it is drying, it should be placed, when perfectly dry, between the pages of a large book. That will flatten it out again. When dry and flat, the stamp is ready to be 'mounted' (stuck in place in an album) or placed in a stock book.

There is no need to soak mint stamps, which should never be moistened as some of their gum will be removed and their value reduced. Some old unused stamps have no gum on the back because they were once stuck down on the page of an album in the same way as they would have been stuck on an envelope. They are, of course, less valuable than specimens which still have their original gum.

Nowadays no collector would dream of mounting a stamp by moistening its back. The usual method is to use a stamp hinge, which is a small slip of thin, transparent, gummed paper. About one quarter of the hinge should be folded over (some hinges can be bought already folded), with the gummed side on the outside. The quarter fold is then moistened and attached to the back of the stamp, near the top. The larger fold is stuck to the album page (tweezers should be used to hold the stamp). Very little moisture is needed: a dab with a damp finger is enough. Too much moisture will make the hinge less adhesive, and may spread beyond the borders of the hinge. With a mint stamp that may result in the stamp itself becoming stuck to the album page.

Hinges are probably still the most popular method of mounting stamps, but there are other methods which some collectors prefer. It is possible to buy long, narrow folders or strips which have a transparent front and a back of some solid colour, usually black. The strips are placed in rows on the album page and the stamps slipped inside. With this method it is not necessary to mark the back of the stamp in any way. That is an advantage for mint stamps in particular as a hinge, however carefully applied, is bound to leave some trace on the gummed side of the stamp. On the other hand, the stamps have to be removed from the slips in order to be examined, and another drawback is that slips or folders are much more expensive than hinges. Most collectors will probably decide that they prefer to spend their money on stamps themselves.

Arranging a collection of stamps in an album may appear an easy exercise. For the new collector with the simplest kind of printed album, it is certainly a straightforward task, even a boring one if a great many stamps have to be mounted. The more advanced printed albums, such as those printed for a single country, offer no problems either, as they have a printed space for each stamp. But most collectors, once past the beginner's stage, will have an album with blank leaves, and for that type the collector must use both common sense and imagination.

There is more than one way of arranging a collection, and it is better to decide how each leaf of the album should be laid out before mounting the first stamp. This is largely a matter of personal taste, and will depend on the type of collection, the type of album, and so on. There are no rules, but some general guidelines can be stated to help the new collector decide how his collection would be best displayed. After all, one of the delights of stamp collecting is just looking at the stamps and showing them to other people.

Young collectors often make the mistake of crowding too many stamps on each leaf. It is much better to space them out, with no more than five or six stamps in a row and not more than four or five rows to a page in an average-size album. The faint printed background of small squares provides a guide to keep the spaces between the stamps regular. As a rule, two to four squares should separate the stamps in a row, with four or five squares between the rows.

Normally, stamps are mounted in sets, beginning with the lowest denomination and working up to the highest. The sets are usually arranged in chronological order; a collection of British stamps would begin with the 1 penny black and 2 pence blue and end with the latest commemorative issue of the reign of Elizabeth II. With each set, which may well be incomplete, it is important to consider the number of stamps it contains before laying out the page. If there are to be two sets on a page, one set of seven stamps and one of nine, you could arrange them as in layout a) over the page. This arrangement is quite neat and logical, but it does give the page an unbalanced look. Most collectors would work out a way to space the stamps more evenly, as in layout b).

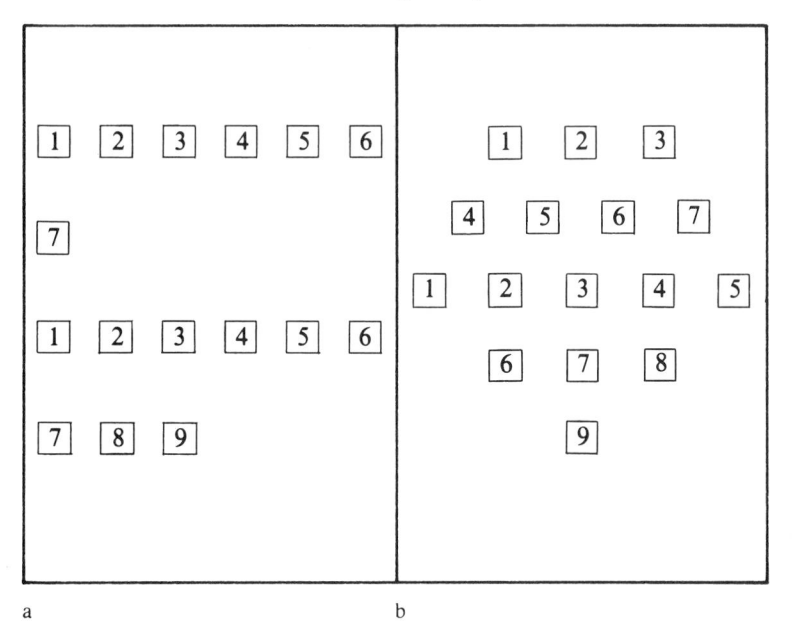

a   b

In most sets, the stamps are all the same shape, but sometimes they are not. In that case they will be more difficult to arrange, and it may be better to ignore the usual order from lowest denomination to highest and choose an arrangement which suits the shape of the individual stamps. Experiments can be made by moving the loose stamps around on the page with tweezers before mounting them.

It is sometimes difficult to decide what to do when a set is incomplete. The obvious solution is to leave blank spaces for the missing stamps. However, if they happen to be very rare specimens which the collector is never likely to own, the blank spaces will never be filled and the page will look lop-sided for ever. Some collectors therefore prefer to leave spaces only for stamps which they have some hope of obtaining in the near future.

In an unprinted album, any information about the stamps mounted on each leaf must be written in by the collector himself. What he writes is entirely up to him. He may write only the name of the country at the top of the page. (Alternatively, sticky labels printed with the names of the stamp-issuing countries can be bought from a stamp dealer.) Probably he will also write the name and date of each issue, and perhaps further details about perforation, watermark, and the name of the printer and designer: these details are given in the larger catalogues. He may also wish to record when and where he obtained the stamps. Some collectors make a few notes on non-philatelic subjects also. For example, if the stamp bears a portrait of a famous person, it may be interesting to record in a line or two who that person was. Other collectors like to draw a small map showing the location of the country whose stamps appear on that page.

There is really no end to this 'writing-up' the collection; but it can go too far. Many collectors would say, quite correctly, that the stamps themselves should be the centre of interest on each page and that writing-up should be kept to a minimum.

Writing-up should be done neatly, and some people feel discouraged because their handwriting is not beautiful. But anyone can write neatly if he takes enough care, and there is no need to develop copperplate handwriting specially for the stamp collection. Anyone who really cannot trust his handwriting can use capital letters. It is a good idea to write the words first lightly in pencil, or on a spare piece of paper, to see exactly how much space they will take.

Before laying out and writing up a stamp collection, it is worth looking at how other collectors do it. There is nothing wrong in copying a good idea, and friends or fellow-members of a stamp club may be very helpful. To see how really fine collections are mounted and displayed, it is usually possible to visit a stamp exhibition or a stamp museum.

11
The
Stamp Collector's
Tools

Some hobbies, like photography or fishing, require expensive equipment, but one of the advantages of stamp collecting is that the tools required are both few and inexpensive. Moreover, none of them is essential. Someone who is just starting a stamp collection can manage with nothing at all - except, of course, some stamps! The first purchases will be a stamp album and, probably, a catalogue. Then, as the collector's interest grows along with his collection, one or two other items will be required (*Figure 34*).

Stamps can be spoiled by careless handling, and the careful collector seldom touches a stamp with his fingers. He uses stamp *tweezers* or *tongs* which, all experienced collectors would agree, are the most valuable tool they possess. A good pair of tweezers costs no more than a box of chocolates. There are a number of different shapes available, but the shape really does not matter so long as they are proper stamp tweezers. Any other kind, like the tweezers used for plucking eyebrows, will not do. They may have pointed or ridged ends which would damage a stamp.

The new collector who buys a stamp collecting outfit will probably find included in the kit a pair of tweezers and also a *magnifying glass*. This is useful for detecting details, errors or tiny tears in a stamp. It also adds to the pleasure of stamp collecting by revealing the beauty of the complicated design of many stamps which is not obvious to the naked eye. Magnifying glasses come in all shapes and sizes and almost any kind will do. Many collectors prefer the little folding glass used by jewellers among others, which has the advantage that it can be placed on the table and the stamp examined through it while both hands are left free.

The perforation of a stamp can be measured with an ordinary ruler marked in centimeters, but a *perforation gauge* makes the job much easier. The standard gauge has scales for between 8 and 16½

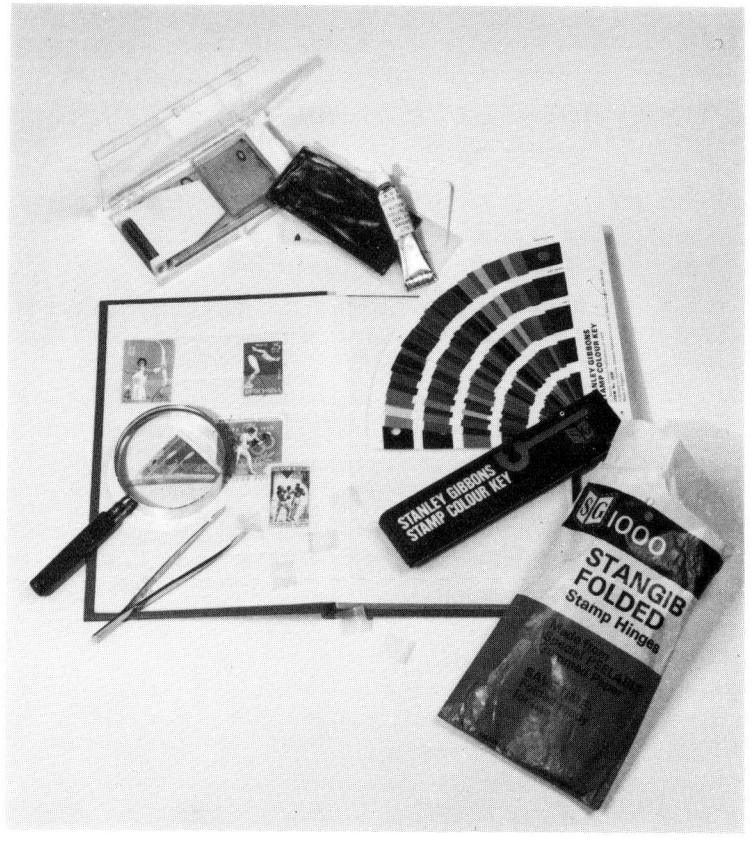

34 Stamp collector's equipment (*clockwise from the top*): watermark detection kit, colour guide, stamp hinges, tweezers or tongs, magnifying glass and stockbook

perforation holes in every 2cm, though few stamps have less than 10 or more than 14 perforations in that space (*Figure 35*).

Most stamp dealers have *watermark kits* for sale. The simplest type consists of a small, black, plastic tray and a little bottle to contain benzine. There is also an electric watermark detector operated by a battery, but on the whole it is less successful than the old benzine method.

The collector checking his stamps against a catalogue is often confused by the descriptions of colours or shades of stamps. What is the difference, for instance, between crimson, lake, brown-lake,

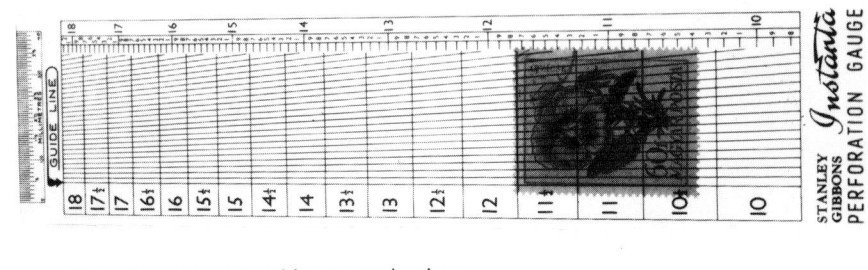

35 Perforation gauge with a stamp in place

carmine lake and deep carmine? The answer is - very little! It is
practially impossible to decide without the aid of a *colour key* or
chart. These are produced by the major philatelic publishers.
Stanley Gibbons, for example, produce a standard colour guide
which contains 100 different colours and another, for more advanced collectors, with 200 colours or shades. By checking a stamp
against the chart it is possible to tell whether the stamp you are
trying to identify is 'carmine' or 'carmine-lake'.

However, this method is not infallible. Colours tend to fade with
age, and some allowance must be made for that when an old stamp
is being examined. Colour charts themselves fade, of course,
especially if left exposed to bright light for a long time. The
collector who leaves his colour chart lying on a window-sill in
the sun may find he has gained a quite new set of colours!

It is sometimes desirable for stamps to be kept for some time
before they are mounted in their permanent place in the stamp
album. Perhaps the collector is not yet sure what they are, or
perhaps he simply does not have time to mount them immediately.
In that case, the best place to store them is in a *stock book*. The
pages of a stock book are made of stiff card with either cloth or
transparent paper strips running across the page. The stamps are
slipped inside these strips. Stock books are made in a great variety
of types. Some are small enough to be tucked into a pocket, others
are as large and bulky as stamp albums. Some are fast-bound, like
an ordinary book, others are loose-leafed with a spring-back cover.
The collector should go to a store which has a large collection on
display and choose the type which best suits his purpose (and his
purse).

12
Forgeries and Fakes

Like paintings, banknotes or antique furniture, postage stamps have often been forged or faked by skilful criminals in order to swindle unsuspecting collectors.

There is a difference between forgeries and fakes which not everyone realises. A forgery is an object that has been made up entirely by the forger. A fake is an object that has been secretly altered in some way to improve its value. A stamp made by a criminal printer from his own printing plate on his own paper is a forgery. A genuine stamp which has been dyed or altered in some way to make it look like a more valuable stamp is a fake.

Stamp forgeries can be divided into three types: philatelic forgeries, facsimiles and postal forgeries.

Some philatelic forgeries are completely bogus stamps, specially made to cheat collectors. There are several examples of 'stamps' of a country which never existed or never had any postage stamps. However, not all these bogus stamps were strictly forgeries. Some were produced as political propaganda. For example, in New York a few years ago a revolutionary group in partnership with a stamp dealer issued several attractive sets of stamps for the 'Republic of Molucca'. The revolutionaries hoped to create this state in territory held by Indonesia, but they have never succeeded. All the same, their stamps circulated for some time among stamp dealers and collectors. Philatelic forgeries also include genuine stamps with a forged overprint.

A facsimile is a copy, and in the past facsimiles of rare stamps were made without any dishonest purpose. Collectors liked to use them to fill empty spaces in their albums when the genuine stamp was so rare or expensive that they had no hope of ever owning one. No deceit was intended, but years later, when the collection was sold and broken up, the facsimiles continued in circulation and unwary buyers found they had paid a lot of money for worthless facsimiles in the belief that they were genuine stamps.

Postal forgeries are like philatelic forgeries except that they are produced for use as normal postage stamps. They are therefore designed to cheat the Post Office, not stamp collectors. In the early days of stamp printing, governments were very concerned that unscrupulous people would forge the stamps, and they went to a great deal of trouble to produce stamps which would be difficult to copy exactly. In fact, one of the earliest postal forgeries was produced on the instructions of the British Post Office, which wanted to find out how easy it would be to forge its stamps.

Many old forgeries are still about, but nowadays most of them are quite easily detected by a collector armed with a good catalogue or a book on the stamps of the country concerned.

Fakes are a different proposition: even experts can be deceived by them occasionally. The simplest kind of fake is a stamp that has been damaged - perhaps torn - and repaired. Careful examination with a magnifying glass will usually reveal repairs of that kind. As a rule, this reduces the value of the stamp to nothing, or almost nothing, and the collector should not buy a stamp which shows signs of having been repaired. Although the condition of a stamp is very important, a damaged stamp is generally better than a repaired stamp. Some very rare stamps, like the 'Post Office' Mauritius or the British Guiana 1 cent black on magenta, are in very poor condition. But no one would dream of trying to 'repair' such scarce specimens.

There are other ways in which stamps can be faked, and as with repaired stamps, the motive is not always a dishonest one. In the past some collectors tried to improve the appearance of their stamps simply because they wanted them to look nicer. However, the collector must beware of such deceitful practices as clipping the perforations to make a stamp appear imperforate or inking in a false postmark.

Among the many stories about fake stamps, there is the sad tale of the St Vincent 1 shilling vermilion surcharged 4 pence of 1881. Only 630 of these stamps were issued, so they naturally became valuable collector's items. Many years ago an elderly collector met a young woman on a train who, discovering that he was a stamp collector, sold him an envelope which had on it the 4 pence on 1 shilling vermilion with a first day of issue postmark. Although the stamp was genuine, the cover, which was addressed to a Mr Howell at the Colonial Bank in Trinidad, was a fake. The unsuspecting collector bought a number of other covers and stamps from this obliging young woman during the next few months. Some time later, when he came to have them valued, he discovered to his horror that they were fakes. He had lost over £7,000 altogether, and the shock of the discovery was so great that it killed him.

13
Errors and
Varieties

Someone who buys an article in a shop and later finds a defect in it will probably take it back and ask for a replacement. But not the stamp collector. A stamp with an error can be a valuable item worth more than a normal specimen. A collector who buys a set of the flower stamps issued by the Cook Islands in 1967 and finds when he gets home that the flower on the 4 cents stamp is described as a 'Walter Lily' will not go back to the dealer and ask him to exchange it for one correctly inscribed 'Water Lily'. On the contrary, he will congratulate himself on acquiring a more valuable specimen. The spelling error was corrected on later printings of this

a

b

c

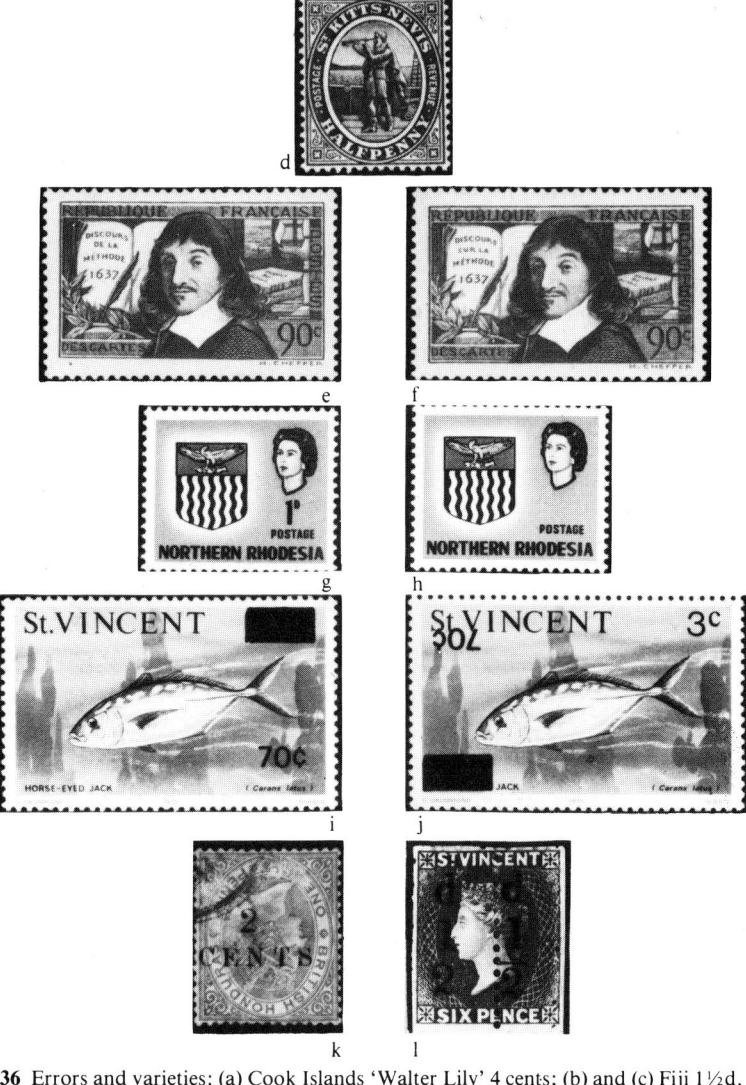

36 Errors and varieties: (a) Cook Islands 'Walter Lily' 4 cents; (b) and (c) Fiji 1½d. with and without helmsman; (d) St Kitts-Nevis ½d with Columbus and his anachronistic telescope; (e) and (f) France 90 centimes with correct and incorrect title of Descartes book; (g) and (h) Northern Rhodesia 1d with denomination missing; (i) and (j) St Vincent 70 cents surcharge on 3 cents, with inverted and misplaced surcharge; (k) British Honduras 1d, overprinted 2 cents, inverted; (l) pair of St Vincent ½d on half-6d, with fraction bar missing in the stamp on the left stamp, so the 'Walter Lily' is much less common than the correctly printed 'Water Lily' (*Figure 36a*).

An error is the result of an accident of some kind during the design or production process. The definitive set of St Kitts-Nevis of 1903 depicted Christopher Columbus looking through a telescope, but telescopes were not invented until after Columbus's death. The 1½ pence Fiji definitives of the reign of George VI showed a sailing canoe passing one of the islands with no one in the boat; in later printings a man appears at the helm. Another printing error is Descartes's book mistitled and then corrected in 1937.

Errors are sometimes called 'varieties', but not all varieties are errors. Sometimes, separate printings of the same stamp are different because of a deliberate change. For example, if a flaw develops on the printing plate and is corrected by hand, some traces of the correction may be seen on the stamps of the next printing. Or perhaps, during the printing of the stamps, one or two sheets of paper are put on the press the wrong way round. This results in an inverted watermark, and the stamps on those sheets are a variety. However, if *all* the stamps have inverted watermarks, then there is naturally no 'variety' as the whole issue is the same. Another common example is a slight change in colour in the stamps of the same issue - the stamps of a late printing being lighter (or darker) than an early printing.

Varieties are collected because they are different, but they are not necessarily any more valuable.

The word 'variety', when applied to stamps, can be rather confusing, because collectors use it to mean different things. Packets of mixed stamps which the new collector buys are often labelled 100 'varieties'. That means only that the stamps in the packet are all different - not, of course, that they are all examples of a 'variety' of the same issue of stamps. Still more confusing is the custom of describing what are really errors, like the empty canoe of Fiji, as 'varieties'.

There have been countless examples of errors and varieties in the history of philately. Some of the most famous, like the 'Post Office' Mauritius, are described in the last part of this book.

14
The
Penny Black

The British 1 penny black of 1840 is the most famous stamp in the world for the simple reason that it was the first government-issued, adhesive postage stamp. At the time no one had any certain ideas on how a postage stamp, or 'label' as it was called at first, should be produced, because nothing quite like it had been produced before. There were two main technical problems in producing a very large quantity of small printed labels: the stamps had to be identical, and they had to be impossible to forge.

However, these problems were not so different from the problems of printing banknotes, and the government asked a printing firm which specialized in banknotes for the Treasury to print the Penny Black stamps. The firm, Perkins Bacon Ltd, is still in existence. At that time the head of the firm, an American named Jacob Perkins, had patented a method of steel engraving with which thousands of banknotes could be produced, bearing complicated patterns but each note precisely the same as the next. The Penny Black stamps were printed by the same method.

A public competition was held with prizes for the best designs of stamp. The Queen's head design was chosen for two reasons. First, it just seemed right. The ruler's head had appeared on coins for centuries, and it seemed equally suitable for stamps. The actual portrait of Queen Victoria used on the Penny Black was in fact copied from a medal produced at the Royal Mint to mark her first official visit to the City of London after her coronation in 1838. The second reason was to make forgery easier to detect. People notice slight variations in a human face more easily than they notice variations in any other kind of pattern or design.

History has proved that the designers of the first postage stamp, by luck or good judgement, found an almost perfect solution. The Penny Black became a 'classic' design. Look at its modern

37 A Penny Black and modern definitives; the basic design has not changed very much

equivalent, in the reign of Elizabeth II, and see how little the basic idea has changed (*Figure 37*).

The stamps were printed in sheets of 240, equivalent to £1 in value. The bottom corners of each stamp were left blank, and a letter was punched into each corner afterwards. This was another device to make things difficult for forgers, of whom the government had a slightly exaggerated fear. Each stamp on the sheet had different letters in the bottom corners. The first stamp in the top row was lettered A - A, the next one A - B and so on. The first stamp in the second row was marked B - A, the next B - B, etc. There were twenty rows and twelve stamps in each row, so the stamp in the bottom right-hand corner of the sheet was lettered TL.

Any forger would find his task very much harder if he made his stamps with different letters; it would take him so long to forge a plate of 240 different stamps that it would hardly be worthwhile. But if he produced his forged stamps all with the same letters in the bottom corners, someone would soon notice that a suspiciously large number of them were in circulation, and the forgery would be detected.

This was a clever device, but it did not allow for the newly invented technique of photography. It proved possible to forge a sheet of stamps by simple photographic reproduction.

Other precautions against forgery were also taken. For example, a water mark (see page 70) in the form of a crown was impressed in the special, hand made paper on which the stamps were printed. Some years later the paper manufacturer John Dickinson (his name can still be seen on stationery) invented a way of inserting a fine silk thread in the paper. Any attempt to remove the postmark from a used stamp in order to re-use it was thwarted, for the thread was broken by the postmark.

The stamps bore the word 'Postage' at the top and 'One Penny' at the bottom. Nobody suggested printing the name of the country; as no other country had postage stamps then, it would not have seemed necessary. To this day, British stamps, unlike those of other countries, do not bear the name of the country, though all of them, even pictorial issues, bear the head of the ruling monarch.

The Penny Black, like other early issues, was not perforated. The user, or the clerk in the post office, had to cut them from the sheet with a pair of scissors. The cutting was sometimes rather careless, and if no scissors were handy, the stamps were simply torn from the sheet; that is why so many surviving specimens have damaged edges.

Although it is always said that the Penny Black was the first postage stamp, a 2 pence blue came into official use on the same day, 6 May 1840. However, some Penny Blacks were issued a few days earlier, and actually appeared on letters before the appointed day.

Black was not a good colour as the cancellation or obliterating stamp did not show up well on it, and in February 1841 the colour was changed to brownish red. Since the Penny Black was not only the earliest stamp in history but was also in use such a short time -less than a year - you might suppose that it is nowadays very rare and therefore valuable. One certainly cannot be bought for a penny, nor for a pound, but in fact Penny Blacks are not especially rare. Nearly 70 million of them were issued in 1840-41 and, although most of them were quickly thrown away, a surprising number have survived. A few years ago a reasonable example could have been bought from a stamp dealer for a few pounds, though recently the price has rocketed upwards. In one catalogue, a mint Penny Black was valued at £38 in 1969 and in 1979, just ten years later, at £2,000. As with all stamps, value depends on condition and other circumstances. A block of unused Penny Blacks, for example, is worth far more than the same number of individual, used stamps. The first sheet of Penny Blacks to come off the printing press was kept as a record in Somerset House in London, and if that sheet was ever put up for sale (which is most unlikely), it would fetch an astronomical price.

15

Bears
and a
Blue Boy

The United States was rather slow to introduce postage stamps. The Act of Congress of 1845 provided for a cheap, standard rate of postage, but it did not make any arrangements for national postage stamps. In Britain, stamps had already proved to be much the most convenient method for prepayment of postage, and as the Federal government had done nothing about it, the postmasters in several states decided to issue their own stamps.

The early postmasters' issues, although not 'proper' stamps as they were not issued by a national government, are very popular with American collectors and are, of course, very rare.

The earliest were the postmaster's stamps in New York City, which appeared for sale only a few days after the new law was passed (they must have been printed earlier). They looked rather like some later U.S. 'definitives'. They were the common size, an upright rectangle about the same as the Penny Black, and bore a portrait of George Washington, the first president of the United States. They were printed in black on paper that appears slightly blue.

Among other postmasters who issued their own stamps was the postmaster of Saint Louis, Missouri. They show the coat of arms of the city, supported by two bears, and are known to collectors as the 'Saint Louis Bears' (*Figure 38*). Equally famous, and even more valuable, are the stamps of Alexandria, Virginia, which bear the words 'Alexandria Post Office Paid 5' engraved in an ornamental circle. They were issued in 1846, and very few of them have survived. Printed in black, some were on brownish paper and some were on blue, but at the beginning of this century no example on the blue paper was known to exist. Then in 1907 a lady in Virginia came across a bundle of love letters which had been written to her mother over sixty years before. On one of these letters was the famous Alexandria 'Blue Boy', probably the only one of its kind left. Odd-

38 St Louis 'Bears' on cover

ly enough, this particular letter contained a message asking that it should be burned, as it contained a family secret. Fortunately, that request had been disobeyed. The letter - and the 'Blue Boy' - survived. It is, of course, almost priceless now. When it appeared at an auction in the 1950s it was knocked down at $10,000, and it would certainly reach a much higher figure today.

One of the exciting things about stamp collecting is that new 'finds' are always possible. Less than thirty years ago a packet turned up in an attic in Ogdensburg, New York, bearing no less than twelve of the New York postmaster's 5 cents stamps of 1845. Nine of them were in a single block, a unique group for this stamp.

Discoveries like that are uncommon, especially when they are entirely a matter of luck. The greatest haul of 'Saint Louis Bears' was the result of quick thinking in a paper firm run by a man called Hemingway. In 1912 the firm was hired to take away a large quantity of old papers from a banking house in Philadelphia. Before the papers went into the pulpling machine, Hemingway noticed that they included a number of old letters posted in Saint Louis in 1846. They were carefully sorted, and a real treasure trove was discovered, no less than 105 examples of the 'Saint Louis Bears'. Moreover, twenty of them were the rare 20 cents issue, probably a larger number than the total known at that time.

In 1847 the United States issued its first stamps, the 5 cents reddish brown with portrait of Benjamin Franklin (the first U.S. postmaster general) and the 10 cents black with portrait of Washington. All the local postmasters' issues came to an end; hence their rarity. In fact the stamps of the first U.S. issue are not at all common either. A hundred dollars would not buy an example of even the 5 cents stamp, and the 10 cents would cost far more.

16
The 'Post Office'
Mauritius

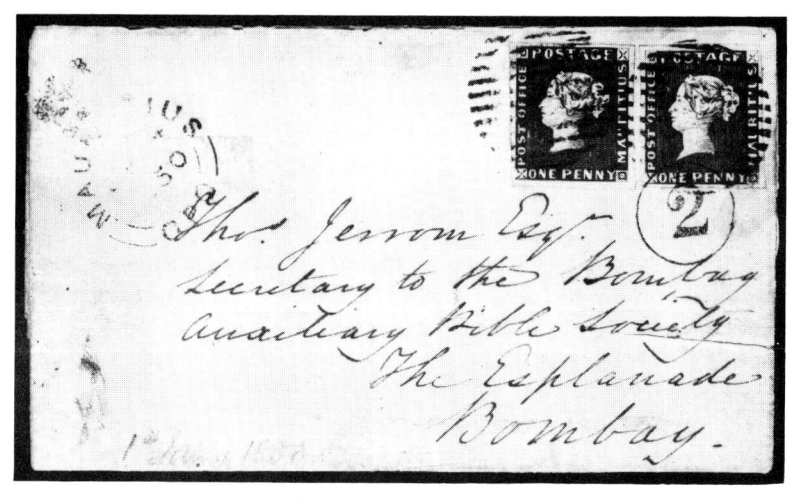

39 Post Office Mauritius, two 1d on cover

After the British Guiana 1 cent of 1856, the most famous of rare stamps are probably the issue known as 'Post Office' Mauritius (*Figure 39*).

Mauritius is a small island in the middle of the Indian Ocean, once ruled by the Dutch, then the French, finally the British. The population includes Africans, Indians, Chinese and Europeans, and they depend largely on selling the fruit, vegetables and spices that Mauritius produces to their much larger neighbours around the Indian Ocean.

In 1847, when Mauritius was a British colony, the colonial government decided that the island should have its own postage stamps. The Governor, Sir William Gomm, when he was appointed in 1842, was displeased to find that communications in Mauritius were very poor. Forty years earlier, when the island was under French rule, it had a good postal service. Sir William, who by the way was an officer in the British army longer than any other man in history (1799-1875), was interested in postal reform. and he was determined that Mauritius should have a better post under the British than it had under the French.

In 1847 the postal system of Mauritius was completely reorganized. An engraver named Joseph Barnard, who lived in Port Louis, the capital, was asked to make 1 penny and 2 pence postage stamps. The design was based on the British Penny Black, with 'Mauritius' along one side and 'Post Paid' along the other. Not many letters were posted in Mauritius, and only one thousand of the stamps were printed at first. Barnard was paid about £20 for his work. A large number of his stamps, perhaps nearly half the total, were used right away for the invitations to a ball which Lady Gomm, the Governor's wife, was giving at Government House.

When the stamps arrived, it turned out that Joseph Barnard had made a curious mistake in engraving the metal plate from which the stamps were printed. Along the left-hand side of the stamp, where the words 'Post Paid' should have appeared, he had engraved 'Post Office'. How this mistake occured is a mystery. Some books say that Barnard was 'half-blind' or at least very short-sighted. He did have trouble with his eyesight later, but he could never have made the engraving (which is of very good quality except for the error) if he had really been 'half-blind'. Anyway, that does not explain why he used the word 'Office' instead of 'Paid'. It is also said that he was absent-minded. Perhaps he was. Certainly, someone must have been rather careless.

But it is possible that the 'Post Office' Mauritius was not an error at all. No one has found the instructions given to the engraver, so we cannot be certain that Joseph Barnard failed to follow them exactly as they were written.

Most early Mauritius stamps are valuable because they were printed in small numbers. Even some of the early 'Post Paid' stamps are valued at thousands of pounds, but, naturally, the 'Post Office' Mauritius stamps are far the most valuable. They are, in fact, extremely rare. Only one thousand were printed, 500 each of the 1 penny red and 2 pence blue. Less than thirty are known to exist today but, like other rare stamps, they do turn up occasionally.

At an auction in 1903 a fine unused example of the 2 pence 'Post Office' blue was bought by an agent for the future king of England, George V, a keen stamp collector. The price, £1,450, was the highest ever paid for a single stamp at an auction. If the present Queen of England wanted to sell her grandfather's stamp, it would fetch perhaps nearly one hundred times as much as George V paid for it. Only one other unused 2 pence blue is known to exist. A used 1 penny red, of which at least twelve are known, was sold at auction in 1976 for over £50,000.

The 2 pence blue in the royal collection was found by chance by a British civil servant while sorting out some old papers. He came across a stamp album he had not looked at since he was a boy, more than forty years before. That evening he showed the album to a friend, who spotted the 2 pence Mauritius. It was glued to the page (no stamp hinges then), and had to be treated carefully with chemicals to get it off without damage.

An even more valuable find was made by a French school-boy in 1902. This clever lad knew about the 'Post Office' issue and he got permission to look through the old files of a firm in Bordeaux which used to have dealings with Mauritius. After a long and dusty search, he found a letter bearing both a 2 pence blue and a 1 penny red. Soon afterwards he found another 2 pence 'Post Office' Mauritius. He sold the two envelopes to a dealer in Paris for about £3,000. Sixty years later the letter with two stamps on it was sold for £28,000, and next time it appears on the market it may reach £100,000.

About half the suriving 'Post Office' Mauritius stamps came from Bordeaux. No less than ten were found by the wife of a merchant there in 1870. Less knowledgeable than the schoolboy, she sold them for a few francs.

17
A Murder
for a
Missionary

Until about two hundred years ago, the islands of Hawaii in the Pacific Ocean were unknown to Europeans. In 1778, they were discovered by Captain Cook, who called them the Sandwich Islands, after the First Lord of the Admirality, the Earl of Sandwich. During the nineteenth century the islands came under American influence, and eventually they became part of the United States. The Polynesian people of Hawaii knew nothing of books or printing until the first U.S. missionaries arrived in about 1820. The first Hawaiian postage stamps were issued as early as 1851, but they were of little use to the ordinary inhabitants, most of whom had not yet learned to read or write. They were mainly for the use of foreigners, and it was through the letters of Americans, chiefly missionaries, living in Hawaii that the stamps became known to the stamp world. For that reason they were given the nickname 'Missionaries'.

The stamps were cheaply produced on a press that normally printed newspapers, and the paper was poor and thin. As a result, the surviving Hawaiian 'Missionaries' are generally in less than perfect condition (*Figure 40*).

Whatever its condition, a 'Missionary' is extremely valuable. Three values were printed: 2 cents, 5 cents and 13 cents. All are uncommon, but the 2 cents, probably because it was not much used on letters going abroad, is much the rarest. About fifteen used examples are known to exist, and only one unused. It was this unused stamp which was the motive for a sensational crime.

In 1892 a French stamp collector named Gaston Leroux was found murdered in his Paris home. There were many valuable objects in the room, including a diamond-studded gold watch, but none had been taken. The victim had no known enemies, and the detective in charge of the case could think of no motive for the murder - until

40 Hawaian 5 cents 'Missionary'

he began looking through the dead man's stamp collection. Under 'Hawaii' there was a 13 cents 'Missionary', a 5 cents 'Missionary' and, next to them, a blank space. On making inquiries, the detective learned that the Leroux collection ought to have contained a complete set. He had found a motive for the murder.

A search for the missing stamp began, but none of the Paris dealers had seen it. The detective therefore concluded that it must have been taken by another collector. Suspicion fell on Hector Giroux, a friend of the dead man and another specialist in early Hawaii issues.

The detective, posing as a stamp collector himself, made friends with Giroux. He expressed great interest in seeing his collection. One evening, carried away by his own enthusiasm, Giroux brought out his Hawaii stamps. He had a complete set of all Hawaii issues up to that time. Among them, the crowning jewel of the collection, was an unused 2 cents 'Missionary'.

The next day, Giroux was arrested and charged with murder. At his trial he admitted that he had killed his friend for the sake of owning the one stamp missing from his own collection.

18
The Cape
Triangulars

41 Cape of Good Hope Triangular (*enlarged*)

Many of the early stamps issued in the colonies of the British Empire were made by the firm of Perkins Bacon, who printed the Penny Black in 1840. All of them are eagerly sought by collectors, and none of them is exactly common. Apart from their age, these stamp are of very fine quality, beautifully designed and printed. Everyone has his or her favourites, but without doubt the most popular are the famous 'Cape Triangulars', the three-sided stamps of the Cape of Good Hope (now part of the Republic of South Africa) (*Figure 41*).

Many countries have experimented with different shapes for their stamps, and triangular stamps have become quite common. But the 'Cape Triangulars' were the first.

One of the problems in designing a postage stamp is that, besides the picture, several words have to be worked into the design - the name of the country, the value of the stamp, and its purpose (usually the word 'Postage' or its equivalent in the language of the country concerned). The name 'Cape of Good Hope' is rather long, and one advantage of choosing a triangular shape was that the sides were longer than the sides of a rectangular stamp and allowed the name to be spaced out neatly along the bottom. (The two shorter sides were inscribed 'Postage' and 'One Penny' or 'Four Pence'.)

On the other hand, a triangular shape presents the designer with one problem that does not arise in a rectangular design: to fill an awkward shape, which grows steadily more narrow at the sides, with a picture. This was the problem faced by the ancient Greek sculptors who made the sculpture for the triangular pediments of Greek temples. The design of the Cape of Good Hope stamps solved it very neatly with a female figure, representing Hope, leaning against an anchor. The design is simple: the designer did not make the mistake of cluttering up the stamp with the complicated ornamentation that, many people would say, spoils the look of many nineteenth century stamps. Tastes change, and today a plainer appearance is more fashionable. (However, the intricate patterns engraved on many stamps were not mere decoration; they also made the stamps harder to forge).

The triangular shape of the Cape stamps was not chosen for artistic reasons either. It had a practical purpose. The African postal clerks at that time were often unable to read, and the point of a triangular stamp was that it was easily recognized. These first Cape stamps were intended only for mail inside the colony. All other stamps at that time were square or rectangular, so the clerks could tell at a glance the difference between foreign and domestic letters.

The first 'Cape Triangulars' were issued in 1853. Anyone lucky enough to own one, or see one, will notice that they appear to be printed on blue paper. This is due to some ingredient of the printer's ink, which tinted the paper. In later issues, the paper has remained white.

A sheet of triangular stamps, if printed in the normal rows and columns, would waste half the plate. To overcome this, the 'Cape Triangulars' were printed in pairs, one pointing up and one pointing down, with each pair forming a square. The technical word for this arrangement is *tête-bêche*.

Some of the most valuable of the 'Cape Triangulars' belong to a later issue. They are the 1 penny blue and the 4 pence red of 1861. In this issue a mistake was made at the printer's with the result that some of the 4 pence stamps were printed in red and some of the 1 penny stamps in blue, instead of the other way around. As the mistake was soon noticed and corrected, not many examples of the wrong-coloured stamps were made, and their rarity accounts for their value. Both the Cape colour errors would probably find a place in a list of the hundred most valuable stamps in the world.

There are many stories about the 'Cape Triangulars'. They played a part in the career of Stanley Gibbons, the man who founded the world-famous firm of stamp dealers which bears his name.

As a boy in Plymouth, Stanley Gibbons was so keen on stamps that his father allowed him to set up a counter in his chemist's shop where, at thirteen or fourteen years old, he sold and exchanged stamps. His brother, who was in the merchant navy, bought stamps for him in all the foreign ports he visited. One day in 1863 two sailors came into the shop with a large bag full of stamps. They had won the bag in a raffle in Cape Town, paying 1 shilling (5p) for the raffle ticket, and they were willing to sell it for £5. The bag turned out to contain 'Cape Triangulars', thousands of them, including many in blocks or strips and some examples of the colour errors of 1861. Although £5 was a lot of money in those days, Stanley Gibbons did not hesitate to pay the sailors what they asked.

This deal was the foundation of his great success as a stamp dealer. He sold the 'Cape Triangulars' at a few shillings a dozen (more for the colour errors), and soon made about £500 profit. His stamp business grew larger than the chemist's shop, and Stanley Gibbons moved to London as a full-time professional stamp dealer. In time he became the largest dealer in the world; he sold the business eventually for £25,000. The firm has kept its place as the foremost British dealer, famous for its catalogues, and it is still called 'Stanley Gibbons'. When it was taken over by a large printing company in 1979, the new owners paid £19 million for it.

19
The
Black Swan

Australia, as everyone knows, is an island. It was not discovered by
Europeans until the fifteenth century and not settled by whites until
the nineteenth century. One result of its isolation from the rest of
the world for such a long time is that it contains many kinds of
animals not to be found anywhere else. Among them is that stately
and magnificent bird, the Black Swan.

The Black Swan was adopted as the badge of Western Australia,
the largest of the colonies which later joined together to form the
Commonwealth of Australia. When the first postage stamps for
Western Australia were ordered from Perkins Bacon in London,
the printers were instructed to make the Black Swan badge the
centre of the design. Only 1 penny stamps were ordered, probably
because the colonial government was already thinking of producing
its stamps at home. Local letters travelled for a penny, but by the
time the 1 penny stamps were ready in 1854 it was obvious that
higher values were needed, especially a 4 pence stamp. Because
of the slow communications between Australia and England, it was
decided to print some 4 pence stamps on the spot.

The Perkins Bacon stamps were engraved, which means that the
original impression was engraved, or cut, in a steel plate. No
suitable engraver could be found in Western Australia in 1854, so
the government printer was asked to print the stamps by
lithography. In this method, the printing surface is flat. The design
is drawn on the flat plate and treated with grease so that the printing ink sticks to the treated parts only; the untreated parts of the
plate remain blank.

For the central part of the design, the government printer took a
transfer of the swan on the Perkins Bacon 1 penny stamps. The
frame around it, bearing the words 'Western - Postage - Australia
- Four Pence', was drawn separately. When the frames were being

42 Western Australia 'Inverted Swan'

fitted around the swans, one frame was mistakenly placed upside down. The result was that when the stamps were printed on the paper, one out of sixty had the frame upside down (*Figure 42*).

These errors are called 'Inverted Swans' although, strictly, it is not the swan that is inverted but the frame. The stamps were printed in sheets of 240, so in each sheet there were four 'Inverted Swans'. How many sheets were printed before the error was corrected nobody knows. Not a great number anyway, as the 4 pence 'Inverted Swan' is a great rarity: only about fifteen examples are known to exist, and they are valued in thousands of pounds.

Printing part of the image upside down is one of the most obvious types of misprint in stamps. There are many other examples. What makes the 'Inverted Swan' unusual is that it was printed in one colour only (blue). When stamps were printed in two colours, they passed through the printing press twice, once for each colour. It was only necessary for a sheet to get accidentally turned around between the two printings to get a reversed image. In that case, of course, the error would appear on every stamp in the sheet.

20
The World's
Rarest Stamp

A little over one hundred years ago a 12-year-old boy in British
Guiana (now Guyana) called Vernon Vaughan was looking through
some old family letters for stamps to add to his collection. He
found one he had not seen before. A 1 cent stamp, badly printed in
black on magenta (deep, purplish red) paper, it did not look very
exciting. It was in poor condition, ink-smudged and slightly
damaged. Vernon Vaughan added it to his collection, but later
he sold it for six shillings (30p) to another collector and used the
money to buy some more attractive issues.

The stamp appeared in Britain a few years later and was sold by a
dealer in Liverpool to Philipp von Ferrary, the greatest stamp collector of the time, for about £150. This was a huge sum to pay for a
stamp then, but when Ferrary's great collection was sold after his
death in 1917, the British Guiana 1 cent black-on-magenta of 1856
reached over £7,000 at auction. (Vernon Vaughan, who lived until
1949, must have kicked himself.) It was bought by an American
millionaire, Arthur Hind, and has been resold three times since. In
1970, it was bought for £117,000 by a syndicate of businessmen. In
the Stanley Gibbons catalogue of 1979 it was priced at £425,000,
but that meant very little. Neither Stanley Gibbons nor any other
dealer can actually sell one because they do not have one: the stamp
found by Vernon Vaughan in 1873 is the sole surviving example.
On 3 April 1980, it was auctioned in New York and was acquired by
an anonymous buyer for approximately £400,000.

In the 1850s not many letters were posted in British Guiana. Probably the Post Office handled less than one hundred a day, so
stamps were printed in quite small numbers. The stamps of this
British colony, like those of many other small countries, were normally printed in England. But sometimes the Post Office in British

43 British Guiana 1 cent black-on-magenta

Guiana ran out of stamps before the ship bringing a fresh supply from England arrived. To fill the gap a few stamps were printed in the local newspaper office. They were of rather poor quality and, of course, there were very few of them. It was one of these that Vernon Vaughan had found among his family's letters.

A few years ago a strange story was going round in stamp-collecting circles. It was said that a second example of the 1856 1 cent black-on-magenta had turned up. The owner of the original stamp got to hear of it, bought it (for a large sum), and then destroyed it in order to preserve the uniqueness of his original specimen. Stranger things have happened, but this is the sort of story that tends to grow out of gossip rather than knowledge. No one has produced any evidence that a second stamp really existed. Of course, there *could* be others lurking undiscovered in some old collection.

21
The Proud
Postmaster

The early postage stamps usually bore a symbol, like the state coat-of-arms, or just figures. Many, like the first British stamps, had a portrait of the ruler. But at that time it was not thought proper to have any other portrait. Pictures of famous men - inventors, artists, etc. - were then unknown on stamps, though they have become common since.

In 1860 the colony of New Brunswick (now part of the Dominion of Canada) changed its currency from pounds and shillings to dollars and cents. It was necessary to change the stamps also, as their values were naturally printed in the old money. The Postmaster General of New Brunswick, Charles Connell, placed an order for new stamps with an American printing company in New York. This was a little unusual, as most stamps of British colonies in those days were printed in England. However, there was no reason why an American company should not do the job. In a way it was suitable, as New Brunswick was changing to the American style of currency.

Five values of stamps were required: 1 cent, 5 cents, 10 cents, 12½ cents and 17 cents. When they were delivered, the government and many of the people were shocked. There was nothing wrong with four of the five stamps. But the 5 cent stamp, instead of bearing the head of Queen Victoria as everyone expected, bore instead the handsome, whiskery face of Charles Connell, the Postmaster General (*Figure 44*).

It was then obvious why Connell had the stamps printed in the United States. A British printer would certainly have questioned the design. In New Brunswick, strong protests were made. The colonial legislature (parliament) angrily insisted that the 5 cent stamp be withdrawn at once and a new design made with the head of the Queen. Rather surprisingly, Connell flatly refused to do any such

44 New Brunswick's postmaster

thing. His face was on the stamp and it was going to stay there. The design of stamps, he said, was his business and no one else's. The colonial government refused to tolerate such high-handed behaviour, and Connell was forced to resign. The new 5 cent stamp had not yet been issued to the public, so Connell, besides losing his job, was disappointed in his ambition to see his own face on the letters of New Brunswick. But, to give him his due, the ex-Postmaster General was a man of grand gestures. He very fairly paid for the printing of the discredited 5 cents stamps, and made a bonfire of them! A few escaped the flames and, needless to say, are very rare today.

22
Back to Front
in
Mount Lebanon

When the Civil War broke out in the United States, all postage stamps held by post offices in the South naturally fell into the hands of the Confederacy. To prevent the South selling these stamps in the North to raise money for the Confederate army, the Federal government declared all the current stamps invalid, and issued a new series.

The Confederacy eventually issued its own stamps, bearing portraits of famous southerners like Thomas Jefferson, John C. Calhoun, and including Jefferson Davis, president of the Confederacy, the first example of an American stamp bearing the face of a living person. But before these stamps could be printed and distributed, many places in the South were forced to issue their own stamps to fill the gap left by the withdrawal of the U.S. stamps. These local stamps were often printed in a hurry with primitive equipment and little skill, and they are not, on the whole, very attractive to look at. However, they are real curiosities, and have been eagerly hunted by many specialist collectors, not only in the United States. Today they are very valuable.

One of the most famous of these Confederate stamps was issued in Mount Lebanon, Louisiana. Like other Confederate postmasters' stamps, it was printed from a woodblock. Great artists of the past have made beautiful prints from woodblocks, and this method was used for a number of very early postage stamps in out-of-the-way places; but it is a crude method of printing compared with steel engraving.

When a printing block is made, whether it is a woodblock or a metal plate, the design must be cut as a negative image in order to leave a positive image on the printed paper. Anyone who has ever made any kind of print - a linocut or a potato cut - knows that the print on the paper is a reversed or mirror image of the pattern cut in the printing block. But the man who cut the woodblock for the 5 cents Mount Lebanon stamps had so little experience of printing that he did not know, or had forgotten, this rather obvious fact. For he cut a *positive* image in the wood. The result was that when he proudly pressed his woodblock on the paper for the first time, he discovered that his '**5**' came out as '**2**'.

The Mount Lebanon postmaster decided that the stamps would do, even if they were printed backwards. They were put on sale and, in case anyone was in doubt of their value, the postmaster cancelled them by writing a 5, right way round, in ink on the face of each stamp.

23
The Canal
and the
Volcano

Some stamps have earned a special place in history without being especially rare or valuable.

At the end of the last century, the government of the United States was keen to dig a canal through the narrow strip of land which connects North and South America. At that time, the only way by which a ship could sail from the Atlantic Ocean to the Pacific was around the southern tip of South America, a long way round if you wanted to go from New York to San Francisco, and a dangerous voyage past the dreaded Cape Horn. A canal twenty or thirty miles long would cut thousands of miles off the voyage.

A canal would be a huge engineering enterprise and required careful planning. Arguments raged over the best route. A government commission had recommended cutting through Nicaragua, but many people thought the shorter, though more difficult route through Panama would be better. There were good reasons for and against both routes.

At that time Panama was part of Colombia, and the Colombian government wanted a high price to allow the United States to take over a strip of its land for the canal. In 1903, however, a rebellion in Panama resulted in the creation of an independent republic which was more sympathetic to the idea of an American canal. It was probably this event which was decisive in the final choice of the route the canal should take.

Nevertheless, there is a legend among stamp collectors that the whole matter was decided by a postage stamp. How did it happen?

One of the arguments of the supporters of a Panama Canal was that Nicaragua was a country subject to volcanic eruptions. The government of Nicaragua, which badly wanted the canal, denied this accusation strongly, and the U.S. supporters of Nicaragua insisted that no volcano had erupted there for many years. Then, one of the Panama supporters received a letter from Nicaragua. The stamp, one of a set issued in 1900, bore a picture of Mount Momotombo, a volcano near the proposed canal route in Nicaragua, belching forth smoke and lava, with people running for safety.

Here was a splendid piece of propaganda. A large number of these stamps were bought and sent to every member of the U.S. Senate together with a note saying: 'Postage Stamp of the Rep. of Nicaragua: An official witness to the volcanic activity of Nicaragua'. Soon afterwards, the Senate voted by a majority of four in favour of the Panama route.

As the vote was so close, perhaps the Nicaragua stamp did have an effect on the result, as the authors of books on stamps say. If it did, it was bad luck for Nicaragua, as the last big eruption of Mount Momotombo took place in 1609! (However, the volcano did produce a few rumbles in 1902 - after the stamp was issued but before the Senate vote.) 'The Stamp that Decided the Canal' makes a good story, though the truth of the matter is that the canal would probably have been built through Panama anyway.

24
The
Serbian
'Death Mask'

The history of Serbia, which is now part of Yugoslavia, has been violent and stormy. Once part of the Turkish Empire, it gained its independence in the nineteenth century under the great Serbian national leader, Karageorge. But in 1820 Karageorge was assassinated by Miloš Obrenović, and that event began a long feud between the two princely families. Although the son of Karageorge held the throne between 1842 and 1858, the Obrenović dynasty remained in power until 1903, when the unpopular King Alexander Obrenović was assassinated along with Queen Draga. The Serbian parliament elected Peter Karageorgević in his place.

With a new king on the throne, the Serbian government set about issuing new postage stamps. To commemorate the coronation of Peter Karageorgević, a well-known French engraver of stamps, Eugène Mouchon, was asked to design the new issue. His design showed a double portrait of the King with his famous ancestor, Karageorge. The government was satisfied, and the new stamps were issued in Belgrade in 1904.

Then somebody noticed something very odd. When the new stamp was turned upside down, a third face appeared, vague but unmistakeable, between the two portraits, and it looked like a portrait of the murdered king. How had this happened? Had some clever supporter of the Obrenović dynasty managed to get at the original die from which the printing plates were made? Naturally, Eugène Mouchon was asked for an explanation, but he bluntly denied having anything to do with it. One rumour going around Belgrade blamed the dead king's mother. It was said that she had bribed the printer to include a portrait of her murdered son. This is unlikely, and the mysterious Serbian 'Death Mask' has never been explained. If the stamp is examined with a magnifying glass, it reveals a face which, though visible, is very distorted. The likely truth is that it was not the result of a sinister plot, but simply a coincidence, like the 'faces' or other patterns that are sometimes made by clouds or the outline of mountains. In the feverish political atmosphere of Belgrade in 1904, it was perhaps easy to see something that was not really there.

25
Maps
into Stamps

In 1918, at the end of the First World War, the state of Latvia, on the Baltic Sea, gained its independence from Russia. It was not to last long, as in 1940 Latvia was invaded by the Red Army and became one of the states of the Soviet Union. But for twenty-two years, the Latvians enjoyed a short spell of freedom.

One of the first decisions of the independent Latvian government was to issue its own postage stamps. They appeared as early as December 1918, when th country was still suffering from the effects of war and its recent occupation by the German army. There was a shortage of practically everything, especially manufactured goods, and when the government ordered the production of stamps, it found there was no paper to print them on.

The Germans had retreated from Latvia in a hurry, and among the stores they left behind was a large quantity of maps, which were no longer useful. The Latvians, however, found a use for them. The maps were printed on one side only, so the state printers in Riga turned them over and printed the postage stamps on the back.

In the 1920s it was possible to obtain a complete sheet of these stamps and thus a complete German map on the back. But it would be difficult to do so now. Individual stamps from this issue may still be bought for no very great sum, but the complete sheets have been broken up by dealers or collectors in order to sell the stamps one by one.

In 1919 Latvia fell briefly under the control of the White Russians (anti-Communists), but in the following year independence was regained. New stamps were ordered, but the old problem still remained - no paper. This time there were no old German maps lying about either. But the Latvians were determined to have their stamps. Other unwanted paper was found, including school exercise books, cigarette paper, and finally paper money. Some obtaining power, but the revolution had never happened and printing was interrupted. The banknotes had been printed on one side only, and so the Latvian government printed stamps on the other side. Like the maps, it used to be possible to buy a complete 'banknote' of the 1920 stamps, but nowadays only individual examples appear on the market.

Glossary

ADHESIVE A gummed stamp as opposed to one printed directly on to an envelope, wrapper or postcard.

AEROGRAMME Lightweight postal stationery designed for airmail use, often with stamps printed on the paper.

AIRMAIL STAMPS Stamps issued for use on mail sent by air.

APPROVALS A selection of stamps supplied by a stamp dealer (or collector), often by post, from which collectors can choose those they want and return the remainder with appropriate payment.

BISECT A stamp cut in half, on the authority of the Post Office, for use at a proportion of its original value.

BLOCK A group of stamps unseparated from one another, usually a group of four or more showing an intersection of perforation lines.

BOGUS STAMPS Unofficial stamps produced secretly to deceive collectors, unlike any genuine stamps.

BOOKLET PANE From stamp booklets (*Figure 45*).

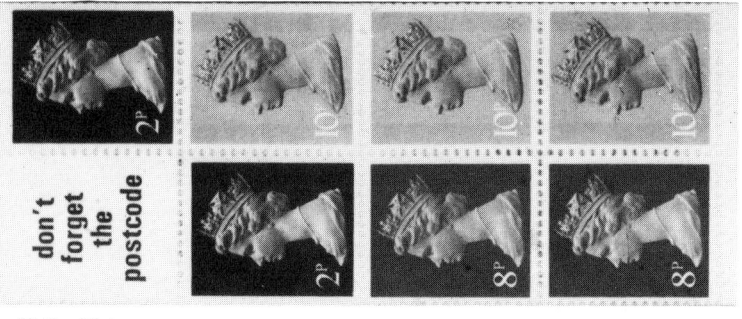

45 Booklet pane

CANCELLATION A postmark or some other mark on a stamp which shows that it has been used for postal or fiscal purposes.

CANCELLED TO ORDER (CTO) A stamp postmarked at the request of the purchaser to ensure a neat cancellation or to gain a used rather than mint copy.

CHALK PAPER Paper given a chalky coating.

CHARITY STAMPS Stamps with an added surcharge to raise money for charity.

COMMEMORATIVES Stamps issued for special occasions such as anniversaries or to celebrate a notable event.

COVERS Envelopes, wrappers, etc.

DEFINITIVES Stamps intended for regular use over an indefinite period, as opposed to commemoratives and other special issues.

DIE The original piece of engraved metal from which a printing plate is made up.

ERROR A mistake made at the time of the production of a stamp. It may be a mistake in the design, the printing or the perforation.

ESSAY A trial design for a stamp.

FACE VALUE The actual price inscribed on a stamp to show its value for postage.

FACSIMILE An imitation of a genuine stamp (not a deliberate forgery).

FAKE A genuine stamp or cover which has been altered in some way to deceive collectors.

FIRST DAY COVERS Envelopes bearing stamps which have been postmarked with the date on which they were first issued.

FISCAL STAMPS Stamps used for tax purposes other than postage, e.g. income tax or receipts.

FORGERY An imitation of a stamp printed secretly to deceive either the Post Office or collectors, or an imitation of a postmark, surcharge, etc., on a genuine stamp.

FRANK Postal mark on a letter wrapper or postcard showing that it is not subject to postal charges.

GRAPHITE LINES Black lines printed on the back of certain British definitives between 1957 and 1961 for use in connection with the Post Office's automatic letter-sorting equipment.

GUM The glue applied to the back of stamps.

GUTTERS The unprinted spaces between stamps (*Figure 46*).

46 Gutters

HEALTH STAMPS Stamps issued by New Zealand and the Fiji Islands on which a non-postal surcharge is added for welfare work among children - a kind of charity stamp.

IMPERFORATE A stamp issued without perforations.

INVERTED Upside down.

LOCALS Stamps produced for use within a limited territory only, not valid for international postage.

MARGIN The unprinted area between the edge of the design and the edge of the stamp. See also *Gutters*.

MINIATURE SHEET A small sheet containing one or more stamps, produced for collectors but valid for postage also.

MINT A stamp in an unused condition as originally sold by the post office and therefore perfect. See also *Unused*.

MOUNTED MINT A mint stamp which has been lightly mounted by a hinge.

NEWSPAPER STAMP Stamp issued for use in posting newspapers only.

OBLITERATION See *Cancellation*.

OFFICIAL STAMPS Stamps produced for the use of government departments only, not normally available to the public and usually overprinted.

OVERPRINT An additional printing made upon a stamp after its original production.

PAQUEBOT MAIL Mail posted on board ships, often marked 'Paquebot'.

PERFINS Stamps which have been perforated in the centre with initials, usually done by private firms as a precaution against theft.

PERFORATIONS The lines of holes dividing the stamps in a sheet which make it easy to separate them.

PHOSPHOR LINES Almost invisible lines of phosphor printed on the face of some British stamps in connection with automatic sorting machines.

POSTAGE DUE STAMPS Stamps used by some postal authorities to indicate that some payment is due on delivery, usually because the sender has stuck on insufficient postage.

POSTAL FISCALS Fiscal stamps authorized for and used as postage stamps.

POSTAL TELEGRAPHS Telegraph stamps authorized for and used as postage stamps.

POSTMARK Any official mark made by a postal authority on a letter or packet by a hand stamp, machine or pen mark. See also *Cancellation*.

PROOF The trial printing made before full production of a stamp.

PROVISIONAL A stamp made for temporary use because of a shortage of normal issues.

REPRINTS New printings of stamps from the original printing plates.

REVENUE STAMPS See *Fiscal Stamps*.

SELF-ADHESIVE A stamp which has a permanently sticky back that does not need moistening, usually protected by a removable piece of paper.

SE-TENANT Stamps of different design, colour, or face value joined together, usually found in booklets (*Figure 47*).

47 Se-tenant strip commemorating 150 years of the Liverpool and Manchester railway (*reduced*)

SOUVENIR SHEET See *Miniature Sheet*.

SPECIMEN STAMPS Stamps overprinted (sometimes perforated) with the word 'Specimen' or 'Cancelled' or the equivalent in another language. They are prepared for various uses, often to familiarize other countries with the design of a forthcoming stamp (*Figure 48*).

48 A specimen
stamp of Antigua

49 Six 6d stamps from Grenada, printed tête-bêche

SURCHARGE An overprint on a stamp which alters (or sometimes
establishes) its face value.

TÊTE-BÊCHE Stamps joined in pairs with one upside down
(*Figure 49*).

UNUSED A stamp which is not cancelled but is not in perfect
condition. See also *Mint*.

USED A stamp which is cancelled, usually to show it has been used
for postal or fiscal purposes.

USED ABROAD Stamps of one country cancelled in another
country.

VARIETY A stamp differing in shade, perforation etc. from others
of the same, normal issue.

WAR TAX STAMP Stamps overprinted 'War', 'War Tax' or 'War
Stamp', used in the First World War to raise funds in some
British colonies.

WATERMARK A design in the paper of the stamp, produced during
the manufacture of the paper.

Index